MASTERS OF ART

REMBRANDT
AND SEVENTEENTH-CENTURY
HOLLAND

CLAUDIO PESCIO

◆

ILLUSTRATED BY
SERGIO

PETER BEDRICK BOOKS
NEW YORK

DoGi

Produced by
Donati Giudici Associati, Florence
Original title:
Rembrandt e l'Olanda del XVII secolo
Text:
Claudio Pescio
Illustrations:
*Sergio
Paola Holguin
Andrea Ricciardi
Thomas Trojer*
Picture research and
coordination of co-editions:
Caroline Godard
Art direction:
Oliviero Ciriaci
Page design:
Sebastiano Ranchetti
Editing:
Enza Fontana
English translation:
Simon Knight
Editor, English-language edition:
Ruth Nason
Typesetting:
Ken Alston – A.J.Latham Ltd

© 1995 Donati Giudici Associati s.r.l.
Florence, Italy

English language text © 1995 by
Macdonald Young Books/
Peter Bedrick Books
First published in the
United States of America
in 1995 by
Peter Bedrick Books
2112 Broadway
New York NY 10023

ISBN 0-87226-317-7

A record of the CIP data for this book is
available from the Library of Congress or
the Publisher.

Printed in 1995
by Amilcare Pizzi,
Cinisello Balsamo (Milan)

Photolitho:
Venanzoni DTP, Florence

◆ HOW THE INFORMATION IS PRESENTED

Every double-page spread is a chapter in its own right, devoted to an aspect of the life and art of Rembrandt or the major artistic and cultural developments of his time. The text at the top of the left-hand page (1) and the central illustration are concerned with this main theme. The text in italics (2) gives a chronological account of events in Rembrandt's life. The other material (photographs, paintings and drawings) enlarges on the central theme.

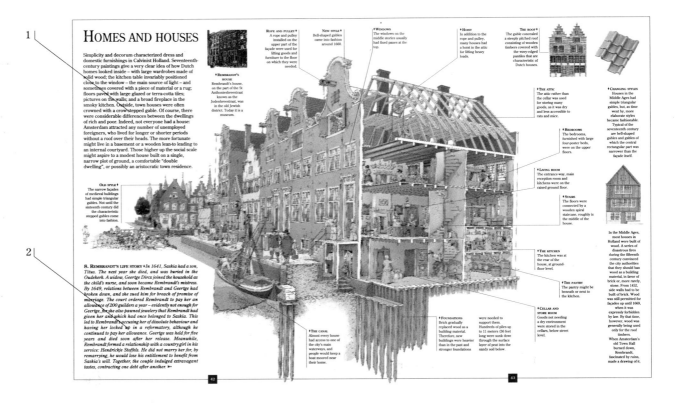

Some pages focus on major works by Rembrandt. They include the following information: an account of the painting's history (1); a description of the content and imagery of the work (2); a critical analysis and detailed examination of its formal aspects (3); reproductions of works by other artists, to set Rembrandt's work in its historical context and demonstrate its originality.

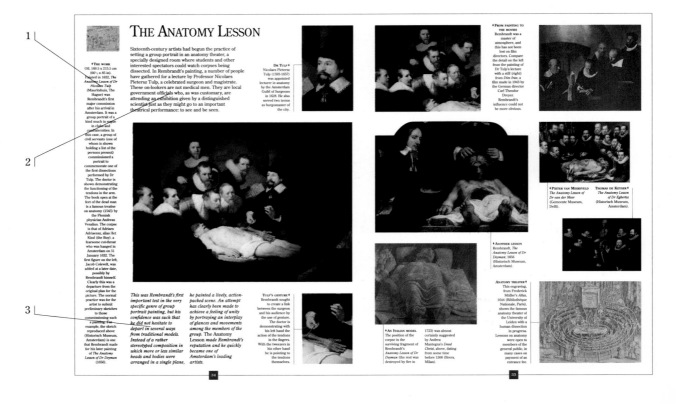

CONTENTS

4 CONTEMPORARIES

6 FLEMISH ART

8 THE SPANISH NETHERLANDS

10 HOLLAND

12 LEIDEN

14 THE MIDDLE CLASS

16 THE BOOK TRADE

18 HISTORY PAINTING

20 ANNA AND TOBIT

22 AMSTERDAM

24 PORTRAITURE

26 A PAIR OF PORTRAITS

28 LAND OF RELIGIOUS FREEDOM

30 SCIENCE AND PAINTING

32 VIEW AND LANDSCAPE

34 THE ANATOMY LESSON

36 FOREIGN TRADE

38 CARTOGRAPHY

40 VERMEER

42 HOMES AND HOUSES

44 GENRE PAINTING AND INTERIORS

46 THE REMBRANDT FAMILY

48 THE WORKSHOP

50 THE NIGHT WATCH

52 ETCHING

54 SELF-PORTRAITS

56 STILL LIFE

58 THE JEWISH BRIDE

60 THE PUPILS

62 KEY DATES; MUSEUMS

63 LIST OF WORKS INCLUDED

64 INDEX

CONTEMPORARIES

Rembrandt Harmensz van Rijn was born and lived in Holland in the seventeenth century. This was a "Golden Age", when the great trading and sea-faring nation reached the peak of its economic and cultural development. The period produced many gifted individuals, including the painters Frans Hals and Jan Vermeer and the philosopher Baruch Spinoza, but Rembrandt remains his country's most admired and celebrated artist. He was an unconventional character and developed a highly original style of painting. In the rest of Europe, the Baroque style had taken hold, but in Holland the prevailing taste in art was for realistic representation. Republican and Calvinist, Holland differed from other European countries in

many respects. Dutch artists worked for a clientele of middle-class merchants and wealthy professionals, and not, as did artists in Italy and Spain, for aristocrats and high-ranking churchmen who acted as patrons. There were some exceptions to this, of course. For example, Rembrandt was commissioned by Prince Frederick Henry of Orange and his Secretary, Constantijn Huygens.

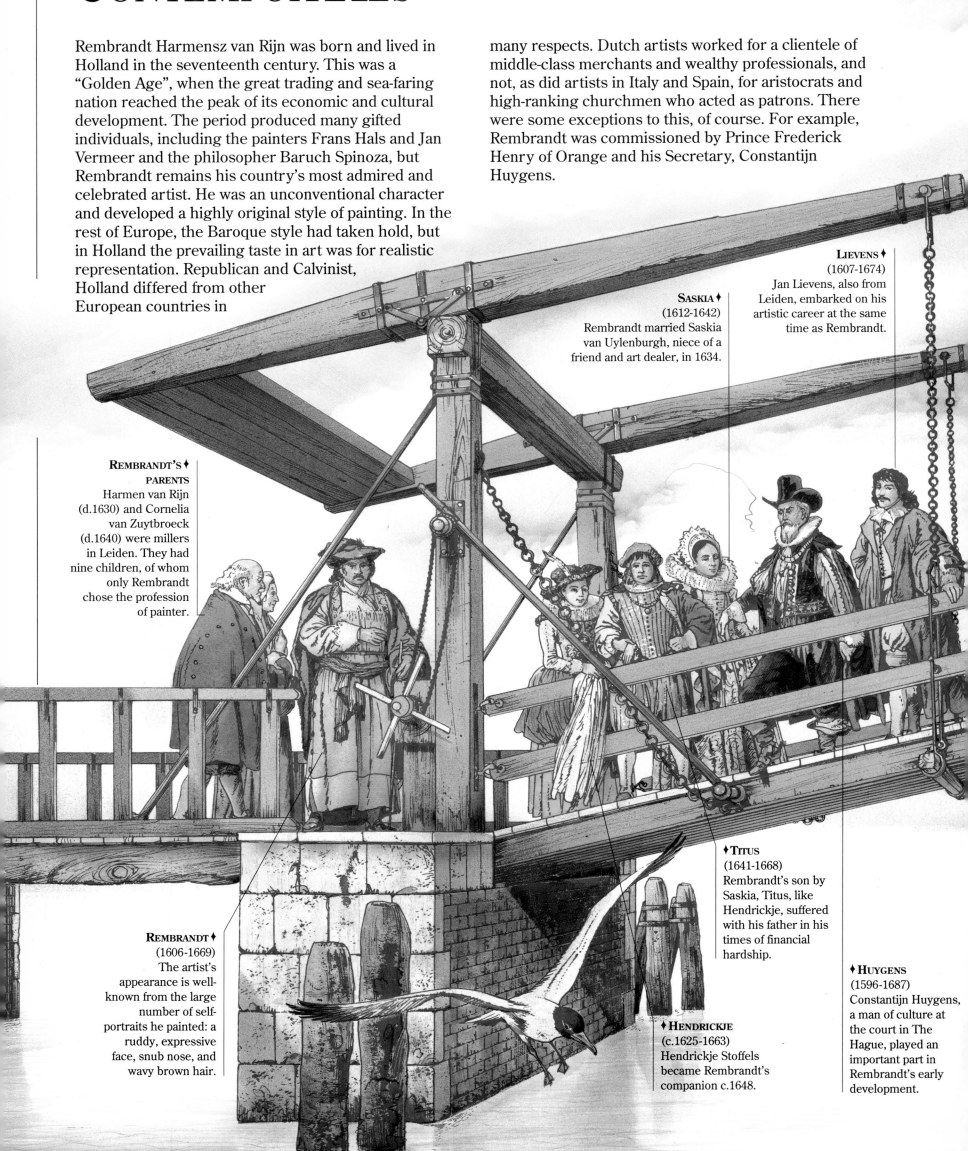

REMBRANDT'S ✦ PARENTS
Harmen van Rijn (d.1630) and Cornelia van Zuytbroeck (d.1640) were millers in Leiden. They had nine children, of whom only Rembrandt chose the profession of painter.

SASKIA ✦
(1612-1642)
Rembrandt married Saskia van Uylenburgh, niece of a friend and art dealer, in 1634.

LIEVENS ✦
(1607-1674)
Jan Lievens, also from Leiden, embarked on his artistic career at the same time as Rembrandt.

REMBRANDT ✦
(1606-1669)
The artist's appearance is well-known from the large number of self-portraits he painted: a ruddy, expressive face, snub nose, and wavy brown hair.

✦ TITUS
(1641-1668)
Rembrandt's son by Saskia, Titus, like Hendrickje, suffered with his father in his times of financial hardship.

✦ HENDRICKJE
(c.1625-1663)
Hendrickje Stoffels became Rembrandt's companion c.1648.

✦ HUYGENS
(1596-1687)
Constantijn Huygens, a man of culture at the court in The Hague, played an important part in Rembrandt's early development.

HALS ✦
(c.1580-1666)
Frans Hals, a portrait painter from Haarlem, is another of the great representatives of seventeenth-century Dutch art.

PRINCE FREDERICK ✦ HENRY OF ORANGE
Stadholder of Holland from 1625 to 1647, Prince Fredrick Henry was one of Rembrandt's most prestigious patrons.

FRANS ✦ BANNING COCQ
(1605-1655)
The Captain of Amsterdam's musketeer militia company was the central figure in *The Night Watch*, probably Rembrandt's most famous painting.

✦ SPINOZA
(1632-1677)
The philosopher Baruch Spinoza was born in Amsterdam. His ideas about individual freedom of thought were revolutionary.

VERMEER ✦
(1632-1675)
Jan Vermeer, a generation younger than Rembrandt, painted some extraordinary indoor scenes.

DOCTOR TULP ✦
(1593-1657)
Featured by Rembrandt in *The Anatomy Lesson*, Nicolaes Tulp, a renowned surgeon, was typical of the emerging professional classes.

✦ RUBENS
(1577-1640)
The painter Peter Paul Rubens lived and worked in the Spanish Netherlands, in an environment quite different from that of Holland.

FLEMISH ART

The art of Holland's Golden Age has its roots in a style of painting that flourished two centuries earlier in neighboring Flanders. The Flemish artists were great innovators in terms of style, subject matter and technique. In particular they developed oil painting. There are many similarities between the art of fifteenth-century Flanders and that of seventeenth-century Holland. In both cases, it was members of a wealthy, cultured and self-confident middle class who created a demand for works of art, to which a large number of painters (though hardly any sculptors) responded. Both schools adopted a distinctive realistic style, portraying the minute detail of their subjects with great care. It was the Flemish artists who led in developing the genres of portrait and landscape painting.

THE MIDDLE ✦ CLASSES
Jan van Eyck (c.1390-1441), active in The Hague, Lille and Bruges, was one of the great pioneers of fifteenth-century Flemish painting. Legend credits him with the invention of oil painting. His patrons included many members of the wealthy middle classes, mainly rich merchants such as this couple from the Italian city of Lucca, dealers in fabrics, whom he painted in 1434: *Giovanni Arnolfini and his Wife* (National Gallery, London).

✦ PRACTICALLY A SELF-PORTRAIT
In the background of Jan van Eyck's *Giovanni Arnolfini and his Wife*, below the artist's signature, is a mirror. As well as the bride and groom, it reflects the painter, standing on the threshold of the room with another person.

RELIGIOUS ✦ PAINTING
The naturalism that characterizes Flemish painting is evident in works on religious themes too, showing that the taste for realistic representation had spread to all sectors of society. In his *St John the Evangelist* altarpiece of 1479 (Memling Museum, Bruges), Hans Memling (c. 1435/1440-1494), heir and successor to van Eyck in Bruges, combines naturalism with intense spirituality.

~~~~~~~~~ **REMBRANDT'S LIFE STORY** ~~~~~~~~~

1 ✦ *When Rembrandt began his career, an artist's position in society was still defined by rules and ideas dating from the Middle Ages. The activities of artists and craftsmen were governed by the old guild system, as they had been in fifteenth-century Flanders. Every city had its own guild, or association, of painters. The admittance of a new member was subject to the approval of his elders, and there were strict rules dictating what prices could be charged, how work was to be organized, and the quality of the finished product. This state of affairs was transformed by the work of independent personalities such as Rembrandt.* ➤

PORTRAITS ✦
This mysterious, absorbed gaze was captured c.1445 by the Flemish artist Petrus Christus (c.1410-1472/1473). The subject of this *Portrait of a Girl* (Staatliche Museen, Berlin) was probably the daughter of an aristocratic family from abroad. However, in portraits in a similar style, the Flemish painters also immortalized the features of ordinary merchants of Ghent or Leiden, professional people, churchmen and city magistrates.

♦ **ATTENTION TO DETAIL**
The portrait of *Giovanni Arnolfini and his Wife* exemplifies several of the features of Flemish painting which are also typical of seventeenth-century Dutch painting: the domestic setting, in an ordinary room lit by natural light; and the faithful representation of objects and other aspects of everyday life: in this case a brush, a pair of clogs, a chandelier and a pet dog – elements which are, at the same time, real and symbolic.

♦ **TANGIBLE AND INTANGIBLE**
The fascination of Memling's altarpiece derives from his great technical ability to render the smallest detail (for instance, the harbor scene behind St John) and the way he has conveyed the spirituality of the figures through their facial expressions. Memling's success rested on the combination in his work of realistic tangible detail and intangible feeling.

FANTASY AND ♦ LANDSCAPE
In the fifteenth and sixteenth centuries, elements of fantasy found their way into Flemish painting. On the right is a detail from the *Hermits' Triptych*, 1510 (Doge's Palace, Venice), by Hieronymous Bosch (c.1450-1516). At the same time, landscape came to be considered as a subject in its own right. On the far right is a detail from a work by Pieter Bruegel the Elder (c.1525-1569): *Huntsmen in the Snow*, 1565 (Kunsthistorisches Museum, Vienna).

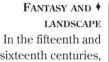

THE SPANISH NETHERLANDS

✦ HISTORY

In the early sixteenth century, the area roughly corresponding to present-day Netherlands, Belgium and Luxembourg was a group of provinces under the rule of the Habsburg emperor Charles V. His successor, Philip II, made the territory directly dependent on Spain, imposing heavy taxes and introducing the Inquisition to halt the spread of Protestantism. Demands for religious freedom, combined with a desire for national independence, led in 1658 to a revolt against Spain.

In 1579, seven northern provinces formed a Protestant league. They claimed their independence from Spain in 1581 but war continued and it was not until 1648 that the Spanish recognized the Dutch Republic of the United Provinces. To the advantage of the north, the provinces of the Spanish Netherlands suffered a decline in the second half of the sixteenth century. The Flemish port of Antwerp was gradually eclipsed by Amsterdam. Apart from a period from 1598 to 1633, when they were ruled by Archduke Albert of Austria and his wife Isabella, the Spanish Netherlands continued under the kings of Spain, who ruled through governors.

In the sixteenth century the countries known today as the Netherlands, Belgium and Luxembourg consisted of seventeen provinces ruled by Spain. They rebelled against Spanish rule and, eventually, seven northern provinces claimed their independence. They became the United Provinces, often referred to as Holland. The ten southern provinces – the Spanish Netherlands – were reconquered by the Spanish king, Philip II. As a result, great differences developed between north and south. In Brussels, capital of the Spanish Netherlands, government was in the hands of a magnificent, Spanish-style court. Holland, meanwhile, developed into a republic. The cultural climate was repressive and heavily Catholic in the south; distinctly more tolerant in the north. Forms of artistic expression were poles apart: in the Spanish Netherlands, a sumptuous Baroque style, seen especially in the work of Rubens; and in Protestant Holland, a sober, middle-class realism.

ALBERT ✦
OF AUSTRIA
From 1598 to 1633, the court in Brussels experienced a period of great splendor under the leadership of Archduke Albert (d.1621) and his wife Isabella, whose portraits Rubens painted in 1613-1615 (Kunsthistorisches Museum, Vienna).

ISABELLA ✦
OF HABSBURG
In 1598, Philip II made the Spanish Netherlands an independent archduchy for the sake of his beloved daughter Isabella. She had married his nephew Albert, former archbishop and governor of Portugal.

✦ THE BELGIC LION
This unusual print, inspired by an engraving from the seventeenth century by Pieter van der Keere, shows the Low Countries in the form of a lion.

RUBENS ✦
This *Self-portrait of the Artist with his Wife Isabella Brandt*, 1609-1610 (Alte Pinakothek, Munich), reveals the refined, aristocratic tastes of Rubens.

A CATHOLIC ♦ CHURCH

In just a few decades, the cultural divide between the northern and the southern provinces became unbridgeable. The Protestant north tended increasingly towards simplicity in dress and furnishings. The Catholic south preferred sumptuous Italianate decoration. The wide difference between the two is clearly exemplified by two paintings of church interiors: one (right) by the Catholic Peter Paul Rubens, *The Miracles of St Ignatius Loyola*, 1618-1619 (Kunsthistorisches Museum, Vienna); and the other (below) by the Calvinist Pieter Saenredam.

♦ PETER PAUL RUBENS

The artist most representative of the Catholic Netherlands is Peter Paul Rubens (Siegen, 1577-Antwerp, 1640). In addition to his work as a painter – his vision enriched by a long stay in Italy (1600-1608), which he regarded as his second home – he managed a large workshop in Antwerp and served the Infanta Isabella as adviser and diplomat. His culture and learning assured him of a welcome at all the courts of Europe. Rubens is the prototype of the Baroque artist, equally capable of painting historical and mythological scenes, portraits and religious subjects.

♦ A PROTESTANT CHURCH

Bare walls and simple architecture in Pieter Saenredam's *Church of St Adolf at Assenfeld*, 1649 (Rijksmuseum, Amsterdam).

SELF-PORTRAIT ♦

This is one of the last paintings by Rubens, c.1639 (Kunsthistorisches Museum, Vienna). He remained one of the Spanish king's favorite artists, right into his old age when he was almost paralyzed by gout.

♦ EXODUS

Spanish repression in the south worked to the benefit of the northern provinces. Merchants, craftsmen and Protestant noblemen moved there from the south, seeking refuge from the persecutions of the Inquisition. This late sixteenth-century painting of *The Sack of a Village* by Gillis Mostaert (Kunsthistorisches Museum, Vienna) shows punitive measures carried out in the south in 1566 by soldiers of the Duke of Alva.

His collaborators included such outstanding artists as Anthony van Dyck (1599-1641). From all Rubens' works, especially his many self-portraits, the image emerges of a confident, cultivated and wealthy man. Great self-assurance comes across in his general manner and in the details of his clothing. This image is very different from that of the seventeenth-century artist in neighboring Protestant Holland.

HOLLAND

Holland reached a peak of wealth and power in the first half of the seventeenth century. The United Provinces were a young nation, taking in the richest and most densely populated part of the Netherlands. The people had paid in sweat and blood for their political independence and were proud of their republican form of government. Their choice of the Calvinist form of Protestantism was another sign of their freedom. Holland's brief period of glory was the result of an exceptional conjunction of favorable economic, political, industrial and cultural factors. As a trading nation and military power, Holland depended heavily on the sea, which was at the same time a threat and its greatest asset. The nation built its world-power status on sea-faring. An urban civilization grew up around its harbors, reclaiming land from the sea and sending forth ships, men and merchandise.

✦ HOLLAND
Holland was in fact only one of the seven United Provinces. However, the name Holland is commonly used to refer to all of them.

✦ REPAIRS
On returning from a long voyage, every ship required a complete overhaul. Carpenters and caulkers would put a vessel on its side to enable them to remove barnacles, replace rotten planks and apply a fresh coat of pitch to the hull.

HARBORS ✦
Harbors were vital centers of commercial activity. Quays were built by driving piles into the sea bed.

INLAND WATERWAYS ✦
Holland's dense canal network was traveled by ships transporting goods and passengers. Boats were fitted with two adjustable lee-boards to enable them to navigate in shallow inland waters and on the open sea.

BUILDING ACTIVITY ✦ AT THE PORTS
Business and trade gave rise to intense construction work all along the Dutch coast. Silos and warehouses were built, and also dwellings for the families of the ever-increasing numbers of workers who were employed by businesses based at the ports.

♦ PORT SCENE
Claes Visscher,
*View of the Port of
Amsterdam*, detail,
1620 (Private
collection).

♦ DRAWBRIDGE
Wooden drawbridges
were a common
feature of the Dutch
townscape, allowing
masted vessels to
pass through.

♦ SHIPYARDS
Dutch shipbuilding
began to develop in
the sixteenth century,
with timber imported
from Sweden and
Germany. A hundred
years later, the
industry was highly
competitive: the
going rate for
building a ship in
Holland was only
sixty percent of the
price charged in
England.

♦ WAREHOUSES
In the seventeenth
century, Holland was
the grain-store of
Europe. The ports
were also crammed
with an incredible
variety of other
merchandise.
Incoming goods were
stored in multi-story
warehouses, where
they were hoisted to
the appropriate level
by pulleys.

♦ DREDGING
Canals and harbors
needed constant
dredging to keep
them free of silt, mud
and sand deposited
by currents. Bucket
dredges were first
used in Amsterdam
in the early
seventeenth century.
Two workers turned
a wheel, which
dragged a chain fitted
with buckets along
the sea bed.

♦ ON THE QUAYSIDE
Processing of
products landed at
the port and intended
for re-shipment to
other destinations
often took place on
the quayside. For
example, it was here
that herring were
salted and packed in
barrels.

♦ HORSE POWER
The bucket dredge
could also be worked
by animals, for
instance, horses, as
shown here.

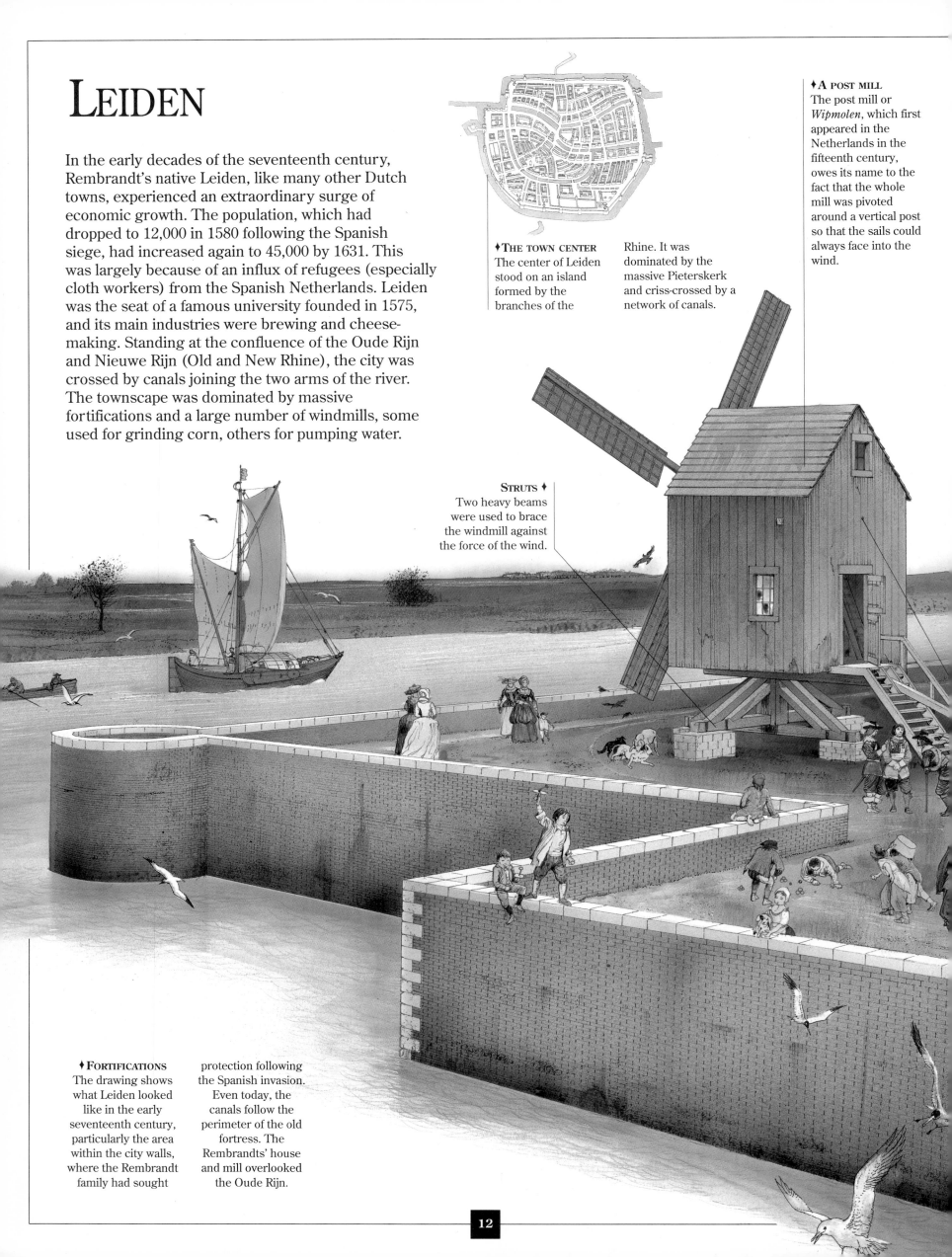

LEIDEN

In the early decades of the seventeenth century, Rembrandt's native Leiden, like many other Dutch towns, experienced an extraordinary surge of economic growth. The population, which had dropped to 12,000 in 1580 following the Spanish siege, had increased again to 45,000 by 1631. This was largely because of an influx of refugees (especially cloth workers) from the Spanish Netherlands. Leiden was the seat of a famous university founded in 1575, and its main industries were brewing and cheese-making. Standing at the confluence of the Oude Rijn and Nieuwe Rijn (Old and New Rhine), the city was crossed by canals joining the two arms of the river. The townscape was dominated by massive fortifications and a large number of windmills, some used for grinding corn, others for pumping water.

♦THE TOWN CENTER
The center of Leiden stood on an island formed by the branches of the Rhine. It was dominated by the massive Pieterskerk and criss-crossed by a network of canals.

♦A POST MILL
The post mill or *Wipmolen*, which first appeared in the Netherlands in the fifteenth century, owes its name to the fact that the whole mill was pivoted around a vertical post so that the sails could always face into the wind.

STRUTS ♦
Two heavy beams were used to brace the windmill against the force of the wind.

♦FORTIFICATIONS
The drawing shows what Leiden looked like in the early seventeenth century, particularly the area within the city walls, where the Rembrandt family had sought protection following the Spanish invasion. Even today, the canals follow the perimeter of the old fortress. The Rembrandts' house and mill overlooked the Oude Rijn.

THE SAILS ♦
A windmill normally had four wooden sails, which were covered with canvas. In high winds, some sailcloth would be taken in to reduce the speed of rotation.

♦THE HOPPER
The miller would empty the sacks of corn into a hopper.

♦THE MACHINERY
A pair of geared wheels transformed the vertical movement of the sails into the horizontal movement of the millstones.

♦ THE MILLSTONES
Corn was fed from a hopper to be ground by the rotating millstones. The speed of rotation had to be carefully controlled. If the stones turned too fast, the flour would be scorched.

♦THE TAILPOLE
By pushing the tailpole on its wheel, the miller could turn the post mill to face square into the wind.

♦ DRAINAGE
Windmills were widely used in Holland because the flat landscape presented no obstacle to the wind. They were used not only for milling corn, but also for grinding chalk and wood and for working machinery and forges. Most ingeniously, the Dutch worked out how to apply wind power to the task of pumping water.

♦THE REMBRANDT FAMILY HOME
Of simple brick construction (stone was reserved for more important buildings), the house was close to the family mill.

2. REMBRANDT'S LIFE STORY ♦ *Rembrandt Harmensz van Rijn was born in Leiden on 15 July 1606. His father, Harmen Gerritsz, was a miller producing malt, the main ingredient of beer. His mother, Neeldgen (Cornelia) Willemsdr van Zuytbroeck, was a baker's daughter. The family had owned a mill on the Rhine for at least four generations and were probably called van Rijn from the Dutch name of the river. It was customary in Holland for a person's name to include the patronymic, a name derived from that of his or her father. Thus Rembrandt is followed by Harmensz, the shortened form of Harmenszoon, "son of Harmen". His father's second name of Gerritsz denotes that he was the son of Gerrit, and Willemsdr is the abbreviation of Willemsdochter, "daughter of Willem".* ➤

THE MIDDLE CLASS

In seventeenth-century Holland, the aristocracy and clergy had less influence than in most parts of Europe. It was the Dutch middle classes who held sway. Professional people and owners of craft workshops and trading companies were organized into guilds – corporations which wielded enormous power in the government of the city. The same type of people made up the city councils and the States General, or Dutch parliament. This strong middle class presented two somewhat contradictory faces to the world. Its members were simple in their tastes, yet ambitious. They were thrifty, yet capable of excesses such as "tulip mania". This contradiction was reflected in the differences between two new Dutch institutions: the Bank of Amsterdam, founded in 1609, was a symbol of security, solidity and conservative caution; the stock exchange represented risk and adventure. The Amsterdam stock exchange, founded in 1608, was a market without merchandise, where individuals and groups came together to finance commercial ventures on a share basis. The percentage they received of the eventual profits (if any) depended on the size of their original stake.

THE NEW TOWN HALL ✦
Amsterdam's new Stadhuis (now the royal palace) was designed by the classically-inclined architect Jacob van Campen. It was built between 1648 and 1665 on a foundation of 13,659 wooden piles.

✦ THE OLD TOWN HALL
Before the seventeenth century, the town hall had been a dilapidated medieval building. It housed the offices of mayor, city officials and sheriff, the city council and the coffers of the Exchange Bank.

✦ THE NIEUWE KERK
The "New Church" was Amsterdam's most important place of worship. Dating from the late fourteenth century, it was rebuilt after a fire in 1645 in the original Gothic style. It houses the tombs of famous admirals of the Dutch navy.

✦ BERCKHEYDE
A detail of a painting of c.1668 by Job Adriaensz Berckheyde, showing daily dealings on the Amsterdam stock exchange (Boymans-van Beuningen Museum, Rotterdam).

THE AMSTERDAM ✦ STOCK EXCHANGE
A meeting place for merchants and businessmen, the stock exchange was built by architect Hendrick de Keyser in the years 1608-1611. It consisted of a simple arcaded courtyard with shops on the floor above.

BUILT ON WATER ✦
Just a few yards beneath the feet of merchants intent on negotiating business arrangements ran the river Amstel. Stock-exchange activities were strictly regulated: the floor was open only two hours a day; weapons, insults and begging were strictly forbidden.

MONEY ♦
Where so much business activity was based on buying and selling, money matters were very important. Many people earned their living from money-changing, banking and minting coins.

♦ THE AMSTEL
Amsterdam stands on a river – the Amstel. However, the water is too shallow for ocean-going vessels of deep draft to be able to travel on it.

Therefore, in-coming ships had to anchor at the mouth of the river and transfer their cargoes to smaller vessels which were able to dock in the heart of the city.

♦ TULIP MANIA
In 1634-1637, people all over Holland invested recklessly in tulip bulbs, hoping they would make huge profits. Prices climbed sky high before the bubble burst, leaving thousands destitute.

♦ WEIGH-HOUSE
One of the secrets of Amsterdam's commercial success was its efficient services, including banking and transport. In 1556, the first public weigh-house was installed in the main square, the Dam. Two more were built at a later date: for heavy goods and for cheese.

♦ GUILDS
Most of the city's business was regulated by guilds, whose members held a virtual monopoly over various occupations. One guild was responsible for loading and unloading ships; another for maritime transport, and so on. Even sack hirers, beer porters and postmen were organized in this way.

THE BOOK TRADE

Holland's Golden Age coincided with a general flowering in Europe of art, literature and the sciences. However, much to the advantage of Dutch publishers and booksellers, Holland stood out from the rest of Europe in that there was no censorship there. The Spanish had introduced strict censorship in the southern Netherlands, making it impossible to publish texts that deviated in any way from the orthodox Catholic view, and this had forced numbers of booksellers to seek refuge in Holland at the end of the sixteenth century. The same pattern of events was to be repeated in the 1680s, when French Huguenots, persecuted in their own country, found a welcome in the United Provinces. The result was that in Amsterdam, for example, the number of bookshops increased from eighty or so to a hundred-and-eighty in the space of fifty years (1625-1675); and the benefits were felt all over Europe too, for the shrewd Dutch merchants managed to meet orders for books, wherever they came from. The bookshops of Amsterdam, Leiden and Utrecht stocked a wealth of publications in all languages and attracted customers of all interests, from explorers to merchants.

♦ BLAEU
During the seventeenth century, two families of printers and booksellers, Blaeu and Elzevier, rose to prominence. Willem Jansz Blaeu founded his business in 1599. Though from a Mennonite background (adhering to a radical version of Protestantism), he published books for Calvinists and Jesuits alike. His specialities were cartography and the manufacture of terrestrial and celestial globes. On the strength of his nautical charts and atlases, he was appointed official cartographer to the Dutch East India Company.

♦ LOUIS ELZEVIER
A refugee from the Spanish Netherlands, Louis Elzevier set up shop in Leiden in 1580, then moved to Amsterdam. He published authors who were banned elsewhere: Descartes, Pascal, Galileo, Gassendi and Hobbes. In 1674, the Elzevier bookshop had no fewer than 20,000 titles in stock. Above, one of the marks that distinguished works published by Elzevier.

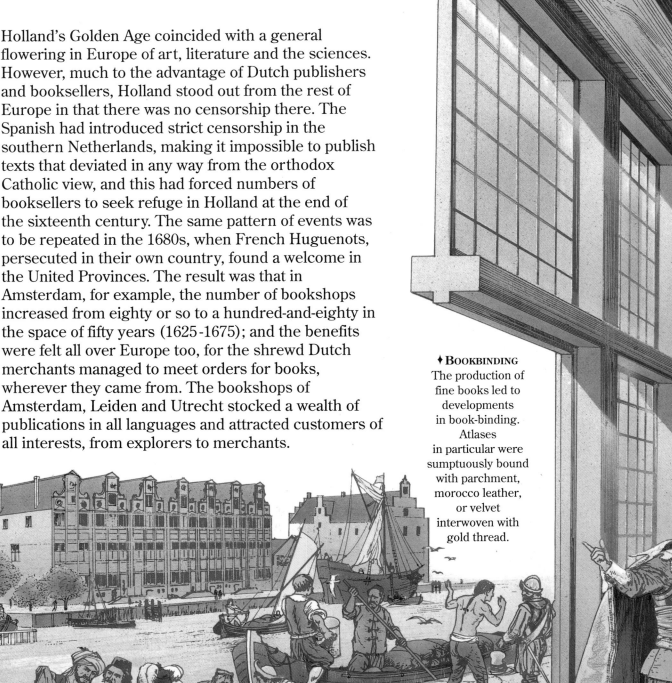

♦ BOOKBINDING
The production of fine books led to developments in book-binding. Atlases in particular were sumptuously bound with parchment, morocco leather, or velvet interwoven with gold thread.

♦ MAPS AND CHARTS
A planisphere (right) and a chart of the Strait of Malacca (left). Both were published by Blaeu, in 1665 and 1653 respectively.

♦ A VAST RANGE
A high level of literacy led to a constant demand for reading matter, encouraging publishers to produce a great variety of books. Bookshops sold Bibles and tracts, large numbers of almanacs, and also popular prints.

In Holland, books were not expensive. Guild regulations were not strictly applied; the royalties received by authors were hardly generous, and when a book was reprinted the author's rights were often not respected.

♦ PRINTING
The activities of printers and booksellers were closely related. In fact the two trades were often practiced on the same premises.

♦ MAPS
Every bookshop displayed a large number of maps and atlases, which were produced mainly by Blaeu and Hondius. The East India Company made sure that confidential information was not divulged: therefore some of the printed maps were not as complete as they might have been!

3. REMBRANDT'S LIFE STORY ♦ *Because the van Rijn family was relatively well-off, the young Rembrandt, unlike his brothers, was not obliged to learn a common trade or follow in his father's footsteps and become a miller. His parents hoped he would enter one of the professions or obtain an administrative post in local government, and so they sent him to the grammar school to pursue his studies. In 1620, when he was only fourteen years old, Rembrandt's name was put down for the University of Leiden: it was quite common to make early arrangements of this kind. However, Rembrandt never took up his place, partly because life at the faculty of theology – for which he was probably enrolled – was disrupted in those years by clashes between opposing religious factions, and partly because he was gripped by a new enthusiasm: for painting.* ⟫♦

HISTORY PAINTING

The genre known as history painting also included political, mythological, and often religious subjects taken from the scriptures or the lives of the saints. In seventeenth-century Holland this kind of painting was not much in favor, surviving more because it was traditional than in response to a real market demand. It was losing ground to genres that were in keeping with the tastes of the new middle classes. They preferred portraits, landscapes or scenes from daily life. However, history painting did continue to find admirers in aristocratic circles and where people were in touch with the Renaissance culture of Italy. Italian painters had made the Baroque style dominant in the rest of Europe.

ALLEGORY ✦
Gérard de Lairesse,
*The Peoples of the
World Paying Homage
to Amsterdam*, detail,
c.1670-1680
(Historisch Museum,
Amsterdam)

4. REMBRANDT'S LIFE STORY ✦ *At the age of fifteen, Rembrandt already demonstrated a prodigious talent for drawing. His father finally agreed that he should give up his academic studies and be apprenticed to a local painter, Jacob van Swanenburgh. Though not a great master, Jacob was a good history painter and taught his pupil the techniques and the repertoire of subjects currently in vogue. Rembrandt stayed in his workshop from 1621 to 1624, and was then considered mature enough to be instructed by a master of greater talent. His new teacher was again a history painter, Pieter Lastman, who had also spent a long period in Italy. His workshop was in Amsterdam, where Rembrandt spent six months. On his return to Leiden, he set up a studio in his father's house and was closely associated with another promising local painter, Jan Lievens (1607-1674), a year younger than himself and no less ambitious. Precocious and versatile, at the age of fourteen Lievens was already an independent painter.* ⟫✦

**HISTORICAL AND ✦
POLITICAL SUBJECTS**
Allegorical paintings
and works celebrating
historical events were
commissioned mainly
by the court and public
institutions.
1. Caesar van
Everdingen, *The
Glorification of the
Burgomasters of
Amsterdam*
(Kunsthalle,
Hamburg).
2. Ferdinand Bol,
*Allegory for the
Admiralty*, detail,
c.1660 (Historisch
Museum,
Amsterdam).
3. Gérard de Lairesse,
*The Peoples of the
World Paying Homage
to Amsterdam*, c.1670-
1680 (Historisch
Museum, Amsterdam).
4. Ferdinand Bol, *The
Courage of Fabricius in
the Camp of Pyrrhus*,
1650 (Historisch
Museum, Amsterdam).
5. Philips Wouwerman,
Battle Scene, 1650
(National Gallery,
London).

**RELIGIOUS ✦
SUBJECTS**
In tolerant, Calvinist
Holland, the purpose
of paintings
illustrating stories
from the Old and
New Testaments was
to edify believers.
Works of this kind
were generally
commissioned by
private citizens as
there was no official
church patronage.
1. Pieter Lastman,
Deposition, c.1620
(Musée des Beaux-
Arts, Lille).
2. Jan Lievens, *Pilate
Washing his Hands*,
1625-1630 (Lakenhal,
Leiden).
3. Pieter Lastman,
*Susanna and the
Elders*, detail, 1614
(Gemäldegalerie,
Berlin).
4. Rembrandt,
Balaam's Ass, 1626
(Musée Cognaq-Jay,
Paris).
5. Gerbrandt van den
Eeckhout, *Christ in
the Synagogue at
Nazareth*, 1658
(National Gallery of
Ireland, Dublin).

ANNA AND TOBIT

The episode represented in this painting comes from the *Book of Tobit* (part of the Old Testament in Catholic Bibles). Tobit, once rich but now blind and reduced to poverty, lives humbly with his wife Anna, who makes a living by spinning and weaving. One day Anna comes home with a kid. Tobit, jumping to the conclusion that she has stolen it, urges her to give it back. Rembrandt has captured Anna staring in amazement at her husband, having proclaimed her innocence. Realizing his blindness is spiritual as well as physical, Tobit asks forgiveness of God and his wife.

♦ **THE WORK**
Rembrandt's first documented work is a *Stoning of St Stephen* (1625), now in Lyons. However, his painting of *Anna and Tobit* (or *Anna Accused by Tobit*), 1626, is considered his first real masterpiece (Rijksmuseum, Amsterdam).
It is a wooden panel, 39.5 x 30 cm (15¹/₂ x 12 in), painted when he was just twenty.
It is clear that Rembrandt had already mastered the technique of showing the play of light and shade in an enclosed room and was more than competent in his use of materials. X-ray examination has revealed that the artist first painted the entire background and the spinning apparatus, and then superimposed the figures of Anna and Tobit.

♦ **ATTENTION TO** ♦ **DETAIL**
The wicker basket in the niche over the door is a real tour de force, the sign of an artist supremely confident of his technical ability.

♦ **THE SETTING**
If you look carefully at the darker parts of the scene, you can see a bunch of garlic and a small cage by the window and various pots and pans on the shelves behind. All such details add to the realism of Rembrandt's painting.

♦ **STUDIES**
An etching and a drawing by Rembrandt:
top: *Rembrandt's Mother*, 1631 (Bibliothèque Nationale, Paris);
above: *Head*, c.1636 (Barber Institute, Birmingham).

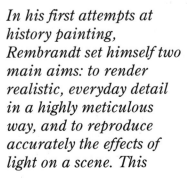

In his first attempts at history painting, Rembrandt set himself two main aims: to render realistic, everyday detail in a highly meticulous way, and to reproduce accurately the effects of light on a scene. This naturalistic approach had the effect of humanizing the Bible story. Rembrandt's painting made it possible for ordinary men and women to identify with Tobit's suffering and Anna's indignation.

LIGHT AND SHADE ♦
Every detail of the painting is highlighted or cast into shade, depending on its position in relation to the two light sources: the window and the fire at which Tobit sits.

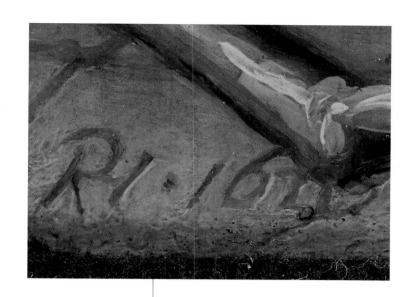

✦ MODELS

Rembrandt's rendering of the story of Anna and Tobit was based not only on his reading of the Bible story but also on the many prints of religious subjects with which he was familiar. Two examples (Rijksprentenkabinett, Amsterdam) are reproduced left: an anonymous engraving of a work by Marten van Heemskerck (top) and another by Jan van de Velde, based on a drawing by Willem Buytewech, 1619. Comparing Rembrandt's painting with these shows how he may have drawn on them as models. In the first engraving Tobit is praying, but the setting is quite different from that of the painting. The second engraving shows a room similar to that in the painting, but with the quarrel actually in progress. Rembrandt's work would therefore seem to combine elements from both scenes. The result in his painting is a silent dialogue between husband and wife, she still stunned by his accusation and he in prayerful suffering.

REMBRANDT'S ✦ SIGNATURE

Rembrandt's early works are simply marked with his initials: in the case of *Anna and Tobit* (above), the letters "RH" – for Rembrandt Harmensz – are followed by the date. Later, he added an "L" for "Leidensis" (of Leiden). When he had become famous (and possibly in imitation of Italian masters such as Raphael, Michelangelo, Leonardo and Titian), he simply signed himself "Rembrandt".

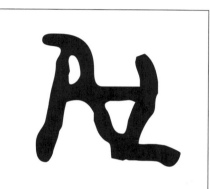

✦ A VARIANT

Rembrandt returned several times to the story of Anna and Tobit, which was a part of the *Book of Tobit* not normally treated by other painters.

In 1645, he painted a panel of *Tobit Accusing Anna of Stealing the Kid* (Gemäldegalerie, Berlin), which catches the old man in the act of railing at his innocent wife.

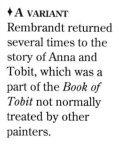

GERRIT DOU ✦

Born in Leiden in 1613, Dou was one of Rembrandt's first pupils, working with him in the years 1628-1631. What attracted him about Rembrandt was his skill in rendering detail. Dou adopted this aspect of his master's work and never departed from a scrupulously naturalistic style. In this version of *Anna and Tobit in his Blindness*, 1630 (National Gallery, London) he took up the subject that was dear to his master, painting it in so similar a vein as to suggest collaboration between the two artists.

AMSTERDAM

Smells characteristic of Amsterdam in its Golden Age were those of pepper from the Moluccas, brine for pickling herring, tar and beer. The city was the greatest market place of its day. In 1631 it was described by the French philosopher René Descartes, who took up residence and had some of his writings published there: "There being nobody, apart from yours truly, who is not devoted body and soul to commerce, everybody is so intent on making a profit that I could spend my whole life here without anyone being aware of my presence". On the other hand, "In what other country could a person enjoy such complete freedom?" In a few decades, Amsterdam grew from an average-sized town to a great metropolis. Its circle of canals was constantly pushed further out, new residential areas were built, and the port was enlarged. Clever use was made of windmills. Before long Amsterdam would be overtaken by London and Paris, but for a short time it was the wonder of the western world.

♦ LAND AND WATER
A fair percentage of the Dutch population lives below sea level. The land on which Amsterdam stands, like much of the rest of Holland (and hence the name Netherlands, or Low Countries) has been reclaimed from the waters of the North Sea by centuries of human toil.
Above: how a dike was made.

THE DUTCH ♦ POLDERS
Polders are pieces of low-lying land reclaimed from the sea. Many hundreds of years ago, much of what is now the western Netherlands was under water. Between the fifteenth and seventeenth centuries, dikes were built to protect coastal areas from flooding and make them fit for cultivation.

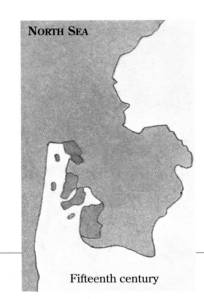

NORTH SEA

Fifteenth century

NORTH SEA

Seventeenth century

AWAITING ♦ DEVELOPMENT
Land awaiting development within the circle of fortifications.

THE AMSTEL ♦

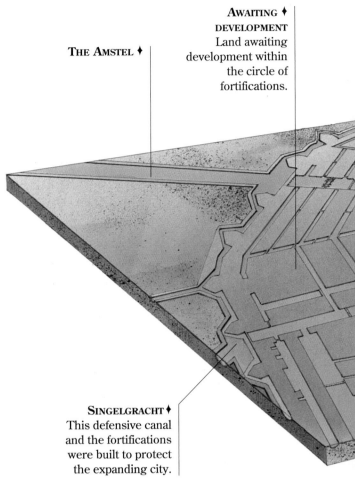

SINGELGRACHT ♦
This defensive canal and the fortifications were built to protect the expanding city.

♦ WINDMILLS
Sea water was pumped out of the newly enclosed areas using wind power.

5. REMBRANDT'S LIFE STORY ♦ *By 1628, aged twenty-two, Rembrandt had made a name for himself as a painter. Aernout van Buchell wrote that the "miller's son" was receiving great praise. In that year too he took on his first pupil, Gerrit Dou. In 1630 Rembrandt's father died and, at the same time, Rembrandt and Lievens came to the attention of Constantijn Huygens, Secretary to the Stadholder, at the court of The Hague. He wrote of the two artists in his diary: "They are already on a par with the most famous painters, and will soon excel them"; a pity, he added, that they have not had the teachers they deserved. Later, he reproved them for not wanting to further their education in Italy, the accepted cultural training for a history painter. In Lievens he noted greater inventiveness; in Rembrandt an extraordinary capacity to register and express emotion. Rembrandt now decided to leave Leiden and venture into a wider market: Amsterdam. In 1631, he went to lodge with an art dealer, Hendrick van Uylenburgh.* ⮞

♦ DEFENDING THE LAND
Amsterdam stands at the confluence of the rivers Ij and Amstel, which was dammed at an early stage of human settlement. Subsequently, a dense network of canals was dug to defend the area from the incursions of the sea.

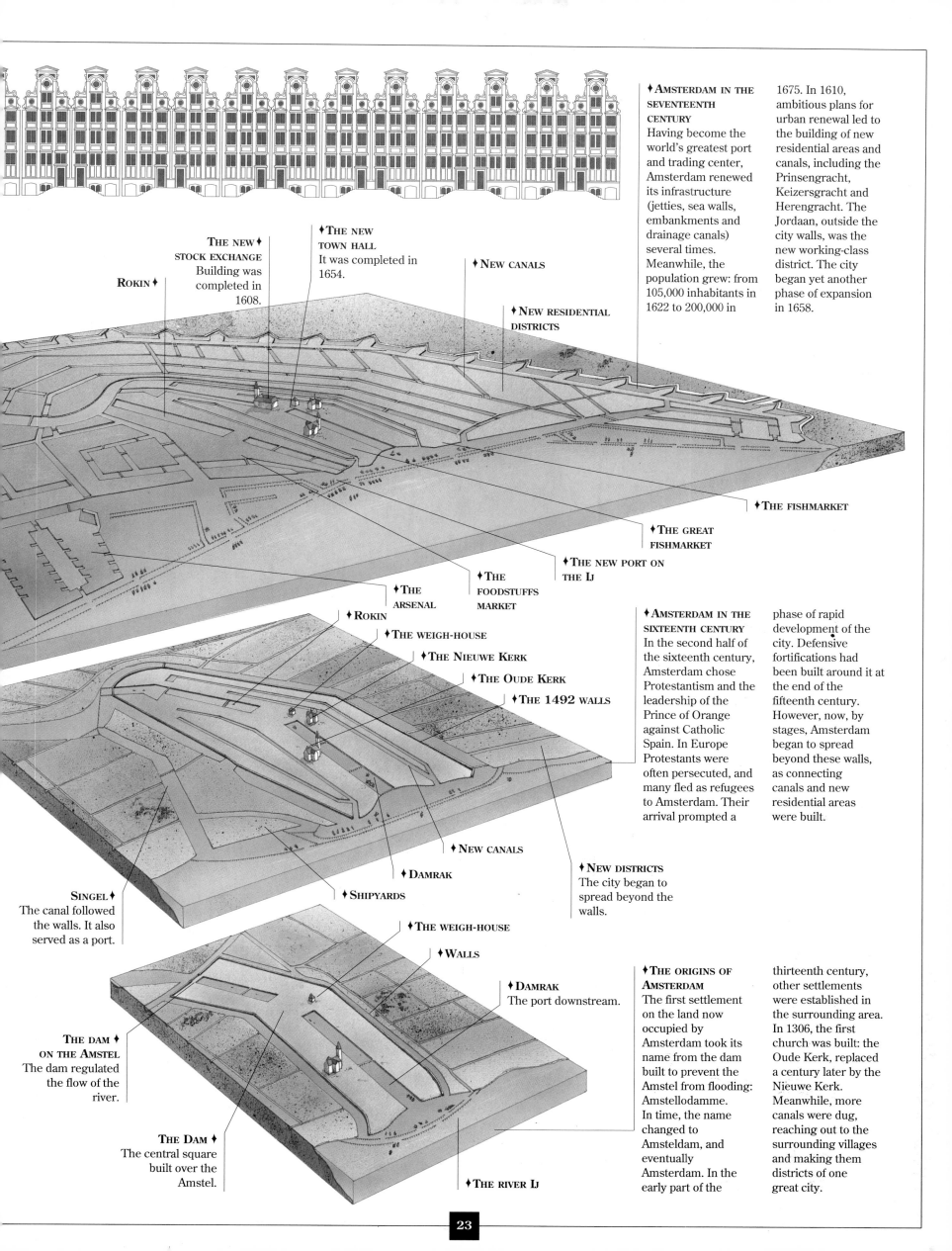

◆ AMSTERDAM IN THE SEVENTEENTH CENTURY
Having become the world's greatest port and trading center, Amsterdam renewed its infrastructure (jetties, sea walls, embankments and drainage canals) several times. Meanwhile, the population grew: from 105,000 inhabitants in 1622 to 200,000 in 1675. In 1610, ambitious plans for urban renewal led to the building of new residential areas and canals, including the Prinsengracht, Keizersgracht and Herengracht. The Jordaan, outside the city walls, was the new working-class district. The city began yet another phase of expansion in 1658.

THE NEW ◆ STOCK EXCHANGE Building was completed in 1608.

◆ THE NEW TOWN HALL It was completed in 1654.

ROKIN ◆

◆ NEW CANALS

◆ NEW RESIDENTIAL DISTRICTS

◆ THE FISHMARKET

◆ THE GREAT FISHMARKET

◆ THE NEW PORT ON THE IJ

◆ THE ARSENAL

◆ THE FOODSTUFFS MARKET

◆ ROKIN

◆ THE WEIGH-HOUSE

◆ THE NIEUWE KERK

◆ THE OUDE KERK

◆ THE 1492 WALLS

◆ AMSTERDAM IN THE SIXTEENTH CENTURY
In the second half of the sixteenth century, Amsterdam chose Protestantism and the leadership of the Prince of Orange against Catholic Spain. In Europe Protestants were often persecuted, and many fled as refugees to Amsterdam. Their arrival prompted a phase of rapid development of the city. Defensive fortifications had been built around it at the end of the fifteenth century. However, now, by stages, Amsterdam began to spread beyond these walls, as connecting canals and new residential areas were built.

◆ NEW CANALS

◆ DAMRAK

◆ SHIPYARDS

◆ NEW DISTRICTS The city began to spread beyond the walls.

SINGEL ◆ The canal followed the walls. It also served as a port.

◆ THE WEIGH-HOUSE

◆ WALLS

◆ DAMRAK The port downstream.

◆ THE ORIGINS OF AMSTERDAM
The first settlement on the land now occupied by Amsterdam took its name from the dam built to prevent the Amstel from flooding: Amstellodamme. In time, the name changed to Amsteldam, and eventually Amsterdam. In the early part of the thirteenth century, other settlements were established in the surrounding area. In 1306, the first church was built: the Oude Kerk, replaced a century later by the Nieuwe Kerk. Meanwhile, more canals were dug, reaching out to the surrounding villages and making them districts of one great city.

THE DAM ◆ ON THE AMSTEL The dam regulated the flow of the river.

THE DAM ◆ The central square built over the Amstel.

◆ THE RIVER IJ

PORTRAITURE

Portraiture emerged as a distinctive type of painting in the fifteenth century. The Italian artists of the Renaissance tended to portray their subjects in a more or less idealized way, while their Flemish contemporaries struck a more realistic, down-to-earth note. As portraits became fashionable in the princely courts of the sixteenth century, the genre came to be practiced by all the leading artists of the day. In the seventeenth century, the nature of the art market in Holland and the moral and civic climate of the young republic led to new developments in portraiture. The growth of a wealthy middle class, determined to achieve social advancement, greatly enlarged the number of potential buyers (and subjects) of portraits. Elsewhere in Europe, the desire to have one's likeness recorded for posterity was no longer limited to kings and queens, popes and cardinals, but it is particularly striking how, in Holland, most portraits were commissioned by members of the middle classes, rather than by the old nobility. Aristocratic ways survived only in the capital, The Hague, where the royal court was in any case not especially brilliant or wealthy. Another important aspect of the market was a change in attitude: in independent, Calvinist Holland, individuals tended to be judged on merit, and for the active part they played in society. They therefore sought to be portrayed as hard-working, worthy citizens, or as members of an established social circle, association or charitable organization.

PORTRAITS OF INDIVIDUALS
Dutch portrait painting was first dominated by the Haarlem school and the lively artistry of its greatest exponent, Frans Hals. Midway through the century, this style was superseded by a more sophisticated form of portraiture, which was fashionable at the great European courts and exemplified in the work of Sir Anthony van Dyck.

1. Govaert Flinck, *Portrait of Rembrandt*, detail, c.1636 (Rijksmuseum, Amsterdam).
2. Frans Hals, *Portrait of Nicolaes Hasselaer*, detail, c.1635 (Rijksmuseum, Amsterdam).
3. Frans van Mieris, *Portrait of Woman with Parrot* (National Gallery, London).
4. Ferdinand Bol (attrib.), *Portrait of Elisabeth Bas*, c.1640 (Rijksmuseum, Amsterdam).
5. Gerard Ter Borch, *Self-portrait*, c.1670 (Mauritshuis, The Hague).

GROUP PORTRAITS
1. Frans Hals, *Couple Out of Doors*, c.1621 (Rijksmuseum, Amsterdam).
2. H.A.Pax, *The Princes of Orange in the Buitenhof at The Hague*, detail (Mauritshuis, The Hague).
3. Ferdinand Bol, *The Officers of the Wine Merchants' Guild*, c.1640-1650 (Alte Pinakothek, Munich).
4. Frans Hals, *Banquet of the Officers of the Militia Company of St George*, 1616 (Frans Halsmuseum, Haarlem).
5. Jacob Lyon, *Captain Hoogkame's Company*, detail (Historisch Museum, Amsterdam).

♦ FRANS HALS
(Antwerp, 1580-
Haarlem, 1666) Aged
twenty, he enrolled in
the Haarlem painters'
guild and soon began
specializing in
individual and group
portraits. He was an
innovator in his fresh,
rapid brushwork,
emphasizing certain
facial features or a
few details of clothing
and leaving the
setting vague and
undefined. His style,
like that of his
younger colleague,
Rembrandt,
contrasted with the
highly polished
manner fashionable
elsewhere.

Hals made an
important
contribution to group
portraiture,
abandoning static,
posed compositions
in order to convey an
impression of
immediacy. However,
the gestures of his
characters are not
always well
coordinated, as they
are in Rembrandt's
group portraits.

**♦ MADWOMAN AND
DRINKER**
Two of Hals's most
famous images are
reproduced above:
The Merry Toper
(Rijksmuseum,
Amsterdam) and *Hille
Bobbe*, c.1630 (Musée
des Beaux-Arts, Lille).

A PAIR OF PORTRAITS

In addition to history painting, Rembrandt soon turned his attention to portraits, for which there was a great demand. He was careful always to adapt the style of his work to the status of the person commissioning the painting: merchant, clergyman, or man of letters (as shown on this page), for which the mood was sober. The pair of portraits here are of two friends, the painter Jacob de Gheyn III (1596-1641) and Maurits Huygens (1595-1642), Secretary to the Dutch Council of State.

♦ THE WORKS
The *Portrait of Jacob de Gheyn III* (wooden panel, 29.9 x 24.9 cm [12 x 10 in]; Dulwich Art Gallery, London), shown on this page, and the *Portrait of Maurits Huygens* (wooden panel, 32 x 24 cm [12¹/₂ x 9¹/₂ in]; Hamburger Kunsthalle, Hamburg), shown opposite, were painted in 1632. They represented a pledge of friendship between the two men, who even stipulated that the portrait of the first to die should be hung beside its companion in the house of the surviving friend. The first to die was in fact Jacob, in 1641, but Maurits only enjoyed the consolation of his friend's portrait for a few months, himself dying in the following year. Constantijn Huygens, brother of Maurits and Secretary to the Stadholder, wrote that portrait painters "perform a noble task ..., as something of us lives on in their work". The portraits remained together until 1786, when they were sold separately and went to different collections.

It is not clear whether Rembrandt painted the portraits for the sake of friendship – in gratitude to the two men or to Constantijn Huygens, his protector at court – or whether he was paid for them. Two details are shown above.

Various styles of painting competed for public favor at this time. Rembrandt employed two main styles, increasingly preferring a free brushwork and seeking to achieve a realistic effect by suggestion.

This was in contrast to the more common style, which emphasized precision and a highly polished finish. The freer, more natural approach was to become one of the trademarks of Rembrandt's work.

SIGNS OF NOBILITY ♦
In this *Portrait of Maria Trip*, c.1639 (Rijksmuseum, Amsterdam), there are many indications that the young lady was from a well-connected family.

♦ FACIAL EXPRESSION
Rembrandt's fluent use of color gives a realistic rendering of facial features.

♦ DIGNIFIED SIMPLICITY
There is nothing ostentatious about the clothing of the two courtiers. Nor does the neutral setting of the portraits give any suggestion of wealth or grandeur.

♦ FREE BRUSHWORK
In this style used by
Rembrandt it was not
necessary to define
every outline and detail
in order to create the
illusion of life and
reality.

A HIGH FINISH ♦
Practiced in Holland
and abroad, this style
relied on the precise
rendering of all detail –
as shown in part of van
Dyck's portrait (far
right).

♦ ANTHONY VAN DYCK
This *Portrait of a
Man with his Son*,
1628-1629 (Louvre,
Paris) is typical of the
work of van Dyck
(1599-1641), who was
from Antwerp. A
painter in the highly
finished manner, he
was so well regarded
as a portraitist that
his services were
sought by courts all
over Europe,
including Brussels
and London.

**♦ HOW THE PORTRAITS
SHOULD HANG**
The light in the
portrait of Huygens
comes from the left; in
that of Gheyn, from
the right. Rembrandt
may have intended the
two paintings to hang
on either side of a
light source.

**♦ PORTRAITS OF
COUPLES**
As Rembrandt
diversified his output,
portraits of couples
became a frequent
theme. Usually the
sitters for these
paintings were
married couples, as in
the above examples:

top, *Portrait of Couple
in an Interior*, 1633
(Isabella Stewart
Gardner Museum,
Boston); and above,
*Portrait of a Seated
Man* and *Portrait of a
Seated Woman*, both
c.1632
(Kunsthistorisches
Museum, Vienna).

LAND OF RELIGIOUS FREEDOM

One reason for Holland's intellectual, moral and economic development in the seventeenth century was that it was a land where people were relatively free to hold different beliefs. Such an atmosphere of tolerance was not found elsewhere in Europe, where each state enforced its own brand of religion and unorthodox opinions were repressed. In Amsterdam refugees were received from all over Europe; Jews were allowed to settle without being restricted to a ghetto. Holland's republican form of government helped to ensure considerable personal freedom. The year 1632 in some ways exemplifies the difference between Holland and the rest of Europe. It was in that year in Italy that Galileo published his *Dialogue Concerning the Two Chief World Systems*; but the Inquisition forced him to take back his support for the theory that the Sun was the center of the Universe. In France, heretics were burned at the stake. In Holland, 1632 saw the births of Jan Vermeer, Antony van Leeuwenhoek, inventor of the microscope, and Baruch Spinoza, one of the greatest thinkers of his time.

WILHEM HENRICK PRINS VAN ORANJE EN VAN NASSOV ETC.
STADT-HOUDER CAPITEYN GENERAEL ADMIRAEL DER VEREENIGHDE NEDERLANDEN.

GEDENCK-TEECKEN HOEDANICH ZYN HOOGHEYT DE II. PRINS VAN ORANJE EN NASSOV ETC. ALS STADT-HOUDER
DOOR DE M. BURGERMEESTEREN CAVALLERY, EN MANHAFTE SCHUTTERS DER STADT AMSTERDAM ALDAER, den 21 Augusty 1672 ingehaelt en den 19 den opgetog't &c.

♦ **THE HOUSE OF ORANGE**
The Stadholders who led the young Dutch republic, beginning with William I (known as William the Silent) in 1572, were members of the House of Orange (the Dutch monarchy today still comes from a collateral branch). This engraving from 1672 (Historisch Museum, Rotterdam) shows William III on horseback surrounded by his predecessors. From the left are William the Silent, Maurice, Frederick Henry and William II.

♦ **SYNOD OF DORT**
In 1618-1619, leaders of the two main Dutch Protestant groups met in Dordrecht, as represented in this contemporary engraving (Historisch Museum, Rotterdam). The Gomarists were rigidly orthodox Calvinists; their opponents, the Arminians were a minority but hoped for tolerance. This time, intolerance won the day, but from 1630 freedom of conscience prevailed in Holland.

6. REMBRANDT'S LIFE STORY ♦ *In the van Uylenburgh household, Rembrandt got to know the art dealer's niece, Saskia, and fell in love with her. She was the wealthy daughter of a magistrate, who was a member of the High Court of Justice of Friesland (the region from which the family came) and had been burgomaster of Leeuwarden. The wedding of Rembrandt and Saskia took place in July 1634. They lodged, temporarily, in the van Uylenburgh house, where the painter and his pupils had already set up their workshop. Also in 1634, Rembrandt received a commission from the Stadholder, Prince Frederick Henry. This was thanks to his friend and admirer Constantijn Huygens, the Prince's Secretary. The commission was to paint a series of pictures of Christ's Passion.* ➡➝

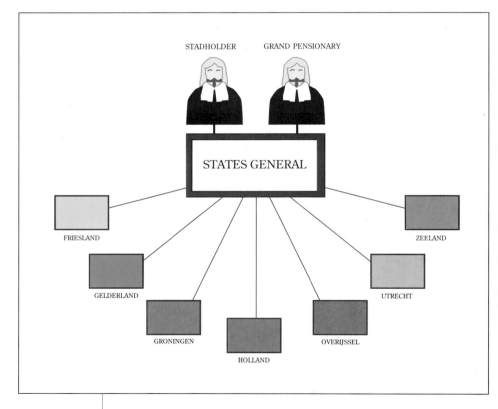

STADHOLDER   GRAND PENSIONARY

STATES GENERAL

FRIESLAND   ZEELAND

GELDERLAND   UTRECHT

GRONINGEN   OVERIJSSEL

HOLLAND

♦ **THE DUTCH STATE**
In the seventeenth and eighteenth centuries, the United Provinces formed a complex federal republic of seven autonomous regions, of which Holland was the most important. Legislative authority lay with the States General, which consisted of representatives of the urban middle classes and of the nobility. The chief executive and supreme head of the army on behalf of the States General was the Stadholder. He often found himself at odds with the Grand Pensionary, a permanent high official who became virtual chief minister of Holland.

♦ GALILEO, 1632

Galileo Galilei (1564-1642) was famous for his studies of the pendulum and the properties of lenses, and for his experiments confirming Copernicus's theory that the Earth revolves around the Sun. In 1632 he published his *Dialogue Concerning the Two Chief World Systems*, supporting the theory. For this, he was accused of heresy, tried and forced to recant. Left, Robert Fleury, *Galileo before the Holy Office*, 1847 (Louvre, Paris).

♦ BARUCH SPINOZA

(1632-1677) Spinoza, a Dutch Jew, developed ideas that offended the orthodoxy of Amsterdam's Jewish community, which expelled him in 1656. He became a great philosopher but made his living by cleaning lenses. In his *Tractatus Theologico-Politicus* (1670), he advocated complete freedom of conscience, arguing that no outside agency had authority to interfere in matters of individual choice.

♦ WITCH HUNTS, 1632

In sixteenth- and seventeenth-century Europe, accusations of witchcraft were rife, made on the one hand by the superstitious and on the other by the tribunals of the Inquisition, ever ready to root out heresy. In 1632, at a convent in Loudun, France, Father Grandier was accused of witchcraft and burned at the stake. In Holland, the last witch was condemned in 1595; elsewhere, the practice continued until the late eighteenth century.

♦ SOCIAL CONSCIENCE

Because of the moral and religious values on which the Dutch administration was based, it was felt to be a civic duty to establish orphanages, hospitals and institutions for the elderly. Left, a detail from *The Regents of the Leprosarium* by Ferdinand Bol (Historisch Museum, Amsterdam); right, *Distribution of Bread at the Almoezenierhuis* by Werner van de Valckert, 1627 (Historisch Museum, Amsterdam).

SCIENCE AND PAINTING

In science and technology too, seventeenth-century Holland outshone most other European countries. The problem of visual perception, which was a central preoccupation of artists, also claimed the attention of many scientists. At this time, great progress was made in the field of optics, with improvements in the manufacture of lenses (of which Holland became the main producer) and the development of the microscope. In some areas, science and painting joined hands, as in the invention and use of the camera obscura. This was an instrument which projected an image of the real world onto a flat surface, so that it could be traced. In fact, the camera obscura did away with the need for an artist to use geometrical perspective in reproducing a scene. The realistic results achieved with the help of a camera obscura are particularly evident in the paintings of Jan Vermeer.

♦ CANALETTO'S CAMERA OBSCURA
A century or so after Vermeer, Venetian *vedutisti* (view-painters) used the camera obscura.

Above, for example, is a view of *The Campo Santi Apostoli* (1731-1735) painted by Canaletto (1697-1768) (Private collection, Milan).

♦ CAMERA OBSCURA
Various kinds of camera obscura were invented in the sixteenth century, notably by Francesco Maurolico (1494-1575) in Italy and Johannes Kepler (1571-1630) in Germany. The device found its application in painting in seventeenth-century Holland, and then in the work of the eighteenth-century Venetian townscape painters, Canaletto, Bellotto and Guardi.

VERMEER'S ♦ CAMERA OBSCURA
For a television program, writer Philip Steadman, reconstructed the room, equipped with a camera obscura, in which some of Vermeer's works, such as *The Music Lesson*, are set.

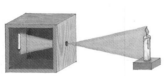

The camera obscura (dark chamber) consists of a darkened room or box with a small hole in one wall. Light rays reflecting from the scene outside this wall travel through the hole, and so an upside-down image of the scene is produced on the inner wall opposite. The image can be improved by introducing lenses and mirrors. This principle was the basis for several ingenious, fixed and portable models. Working in the dark, the operator would trace the trembling, indistinct image onto a sheet of paper.

A PROJECTED ♦ IMAGE
The scenes for which Vermeer is thought to have used a camera obscura are all painted from the same viewpoint. He would be positioned inside the camera obscura at one end of the room and would see, on the inner wall of the camera, an upside-down image of the people and furniture at the opposite end of the room. He would trace the image as the basis for his painting.

Van Hoogstraten's ✦ box
Samuel van Hoogstraten, a pupil of Rembrandt, was famous for his "magic boxes". He cunningly assembled painted images and used exaggerated perspective effects to create the illusion of three-dimensional space. Right, *View of the Interior of a Dutch House* (National Gallery, London).

The Music Lesson ✦
This painting by Jan Vermeer, c.1664 (Buckingham Palace, London), was most probably done in a room similar to the one reconstructed on this page. Signs that a camera obscura was used are the almost "photographic" rendering of details in the foreground, the sparkling colors and the realistic perspective.

VIEW AND LANDSCAPE

Large numbers of Dutch landscape paintings from the seventeenth century are to be found today in museums, art galleries and private collections. The quantity of them is proof of how popular the genre was in Holland at that time. Landscapes, like still lifes or everyday scenes, were greatly prized as items of furnishing and would be hung in prominent positions in the homes of middle-class Dutch families. Landscapes were also far less expensive than other kinds of painting – which meant that landscape artists often had to take other jobs to make ends meet. Dutch landscape painters did not attempt to elevate their art by introducing difficult symbolic meanings, but produced natural, realistic pictures of the towns and countryside in which they lived. This is what the public liked and bought.

CITY SIGHTS ✦
"How life-like!" Words to warm the heart of any Dutch painter.

1. Jan van der Heyden, *View of the Town Hall*, 1668 (Louvre, Paris).
2. Jacob van Ruysdael, *View of Haarlem* (Gemäldegalerie, Berlin).
3. Rembrandt, *View of Amsterdam*, (Rijksmuseum, Amsterdam).

✦BIRD'S-EYE VIEW
View-painting often came close to cartography, as in this extraordinarily skillful *View of Amsterdam* painted by Jan Christiaensz Micker (Historisch Museum, Amsterdam). It shows the city overshadowed by invisible clouds.

WATER ✦
An element familiar to every Dutch person, water is rarely missing from any Dutch landscape or townscape.

1. Hendrick Vroom, *The Port of Amsterdam*, detail (Schlessheim Castle, Bavaria).
2. Salomon van Ruysdael, *Landscape with River,* 1649 (Rijksmuseum, Amsterdam).
3. Willem van de Velde, *The Port of Amsterdam*, detail, 1686 (Historisch Museum, Amsterdam).

7. REMBRANDT'S LIFE STORY ✦ *In 1635, Rembrandt and Saskia moved temporarily to a new house. As his business was growing, Rembrandt also had to look for a new workshop. He found what he wanted by the Bloemgracht: an old warehouse, which he transformed to meet his own needs and those of his pupils, who lived and worked on the premises. Meanwhile, Rembrandt was enjoying a lavish lifestyle. He collected paintings and engravings and bought antiques, prompting Saskia's relations to accuse him of squandering his wife's inheritance. His view was that these items were part of his flourishing professional work. On 1 May 1639, the couple finally moved to a fine house on the St Anthoniesbreestraat. ➤*

COUNTRYSIDE ✦
Seventeenth-century Holland was the most urbanized nation of the time. Although the vast majority of Dutch people lived in cities or small towns, they were keenly aware of the value of land reclaimed from the sea and the marshes.
1. Herman van Swanevelt, *Landscape with Figures*, detail, c.1640 (Uffizi Gallery, Florence).
2. Paulus Potter, *The Bull*, 1647 (Maurits-huis, The Hague).
3. Rembrandt, *Landscape with Bridge*, c.1640 (Rijksmuseum, Amsterdam).

3

3

WINTER ✦

The severe winters typical of the Dutch climate are another common feature of landscape painting. Many scenes of everyday life in winter show how people spent their time when normal work was suspended. For example, a frozen canal prevented navigation, and therefore trade had to stop.

Hendrick Avercamp, *Winter Scene*, detail, c.1608 (Rijksmuseum, Amsterdam).

THE ANATOMY LESSON

Sixteenth-century artists had begun the practice of setting a group portrait in an anatomy theater, a specially designed room where students and other interested spectators could watch corpses being dissected. In Rembrandt's painting, a number of people have gathered for a lecture by Professor Nicolaes Pietersz Tulp, a celebrated surgeon and magistrate. These on-lookers are not medical men. They are local government officials who, as was customary, are attending an exhibition given by a distinguished scientist just as they might go to an important theatrical performance: to see and be seen.

✦ DR TULP ✦
Nicolaes Pietersz Tulp (1593-1657) was appointed lecturer in anatomy by the Amsterdam Guild of Surgeons in 1628. He also served two terms as burgomaster of the city.

✦ THE WORK
Oil, 169.5 x 215.5 cm (66½ x 85 in). Painted in 1632, *The Anatomy Lesson of Dr Nicolaes Tulp* (Mauritshuis, The Hague) was Rembrandt's first major commission after his arrival in Amsterdam. It was a group portrait of a kind much in vogue in clubs and confraternities. In this case, a group of civil servants (one of whom is shown holding a list of the persons present) commissioned a portrait to commemorate one of the first dissections performed by Dr Tulp. The doctor is shown demonstrating the functioning of the tendons in the arm. The book open at the feet of the dead man is a famous treatise on anatomy (1543) by the Flemish physician Andreas Vesalius. The corpse is that of Adriaen Adriaensz, alias Het Kind (the Boy), a fearsome cut-throat who was hanged in Amsterdam on 31 January 1632. The first figure on the left, Jacob Colevelt, was added at a later date, possibly by Rembrandt himself. Clearly this was a departure from the original plan for the picture. The normal practice was for the artist to submit preliminary sketches to those commissioning such a painting. For example, the sketch reproduced above (Historisch Museum, Amsterdam) is one that Rembrandt made for his later painting of *The Anatomy Lesson of Dr Deyman* (1656).

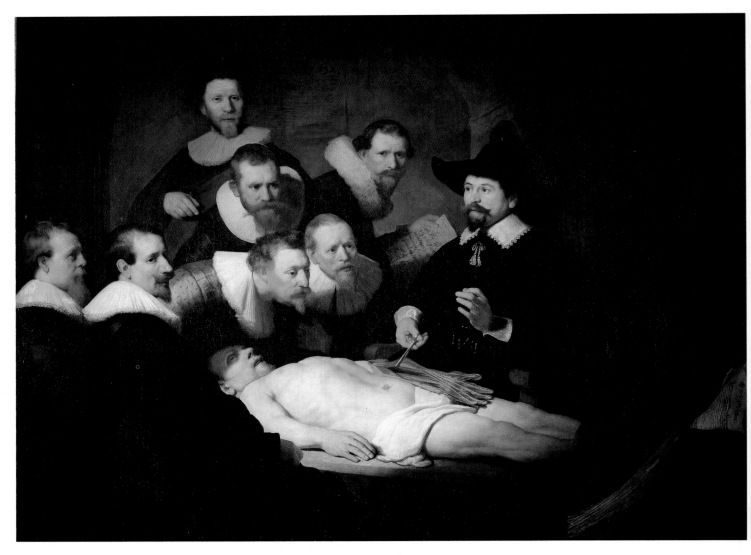

This was Rembrandt's first important test in the very specific genre of group portrait painting, but his confidence was such that he did not hesitate to depart in several ways from traditional models. Instead of a rather stereotyped composition in which more or less similar heads and bodies were arranged in a single plane, *he painted a lively, action-packed scene. An attempt has clearly been made to achieve a feeling of unity by portraying an interplay of glances and movements among the members of the group.* The Anatomy Lesson *made Rembrandt's reputation and he quickly became one of Amsterdam's leading artists.*

TULP'S GESTURE ✦
Rembrandt sought to create a link between the surgeon and his audience by the use of gesture. The doctor is demonstrating with his left hand the action of the tendons in the fingers. With the tweezers in his other hand he is pointing to the tendons themselves.

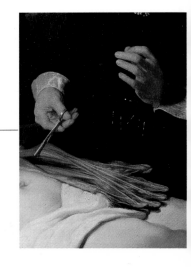

♦ **FROM PAINTING TO THE MOVIES**
Rembrandt was a master of atmosphere, and this has not been lost on film directors. Compare the detail on the left from the painting of Dr Tulp's lecture with a still (right) from *Dies Irae*, a film made in 1943 by the German director Carl Theodor Dreyer. Rembrandt's influence could not be more obvious.

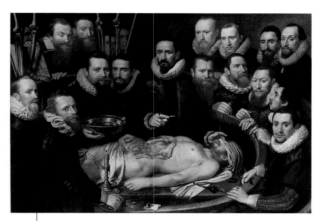

♦ **PIETER VAN MIEREVELD**
The Anatomy Lesson of Dr van der Meer (Gemeente Museum, Delft).

THOMAS DE KEYSER ♦
The Anatomy Lesson of Dr Egbertsz (Historisch Museum, Amsterdam).

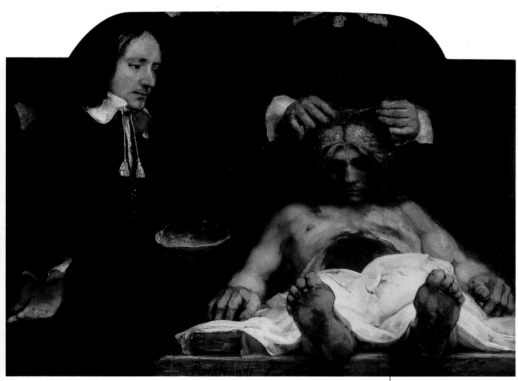

♦ **ANOTHER LESSON**
Rembrandt, *The Anatomy Lesson of Dr Deyman*, 1656 (Historisch Museum, Amsterdam).

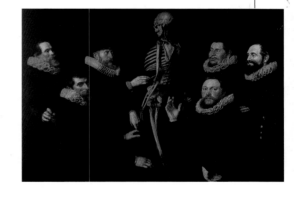

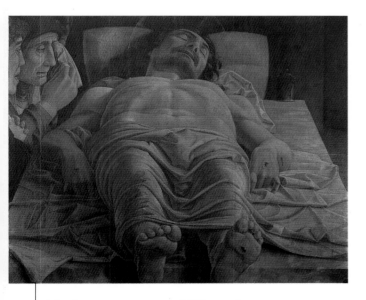

♦ **AN ITALIAN MODEL**
The position of the corpse in the surviving fragment of Rembrandt's *Anatomy Lesson of Dr Deyman* (the rest was destroyed by fire in 1723) was almost certainly suggested by Andrea Mantegna's *Dead Christ*, above, dating from some time before 1506 (Brera, Milan).

ANATOMY THEATER ♦
This engraving, from Frederick Müller's *Atlas*, 1644 (Bibliothèque Nationale, Paris), shows the famous anatomy theater of the University of Leiden with a human dissection in progress. Lessons on anatomy were open to members of the general public, in many cases on payment of an entrance fee.

FOREIGN TRADE

The great geographical discoveries of the sixteenth century led to an enormous expansion of international trade. Ships began to venture across the oceans, beyond the narrow confines of the North Sea, Baltic and Mediterranean. With the decline of the port of Antwerp in the late sixteenth century and the arrival in Holland of specialized workers from the southern Netherlands, Dutch shipping companies also began plying the great ocean routes. Fabrics, timber, herring, spices, grain ... the Dutch were involved in every branch of commerce. Their goods were in demand all over the world because of a competitive pricing policy. Although the wages of a laborer or sailor were higher in Holland than elsewhere, the Dutch took full advantage of the availability of capital and of efficient new technology. A growing import trade, the manufacture of cannon, and a high level of productivity in many activities, starting with fishing and the salting of herring, gave Holland mastery of the seas. Two great enterprises – the Dutch West India Company and the even more powerful East India Company – were the instruments of Dutch sea power.

♦ ARTILLERY PIECES
Sixteenth-century cannon manufacturers were torn between making their gun barrels from brass, which was of high quality but very expensive, and using iron, which was inferior at this time. One-piece, cast-iron barrels were as yet unknown; the barrel was cast in two parts which were then clamped together. The Dutch needed to arm their ships because of the conflict with Spain during the seventeenth century, and this spurred them on to become innovators in cannon technology. The guns were actually made in Sweden, whose iron ore and timber resources were exploited by Dutch entrepreneurs.

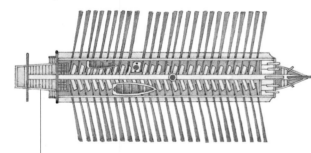

♦ THE GALLEY
In the sixteenth century, a great deal of Mediterranean merchandise was still carried by galleys, ships with one or more banks of oars rowed by prisoners. Galleys were also used in battle, but were made obsolete by ocean-going galleons.

THE DUTCH FLUYT ♦
In 1595, a new type of ship made its appearance in Dutch ports. The fluyt was a fast, three-masted vessel of shallow draft (to enable it to negotiate tricky harbors), and could be handled by a small crew. Its rotund shape, with bulging sides and a remarkably small deck, had two advantages. It gave the fluyt considerable carrying capacity and also limited the amount of tax the ship had to pay for using the Sund (the narrow strait between Scandinavia and Denmark). The amount of tax that any ship had to pay was calculated on the basis of its deck area.

♦ THE GALLEON
The most important sailing ship, for the whole of the sixteenth century and part of the seventeenth, was the galleon. It was a two-decker with three masts and a bowsprit. Generally fitted out for war, it carried a powerful armament of cannon. In 1588 English galleons had defeated the Spanish Armada.

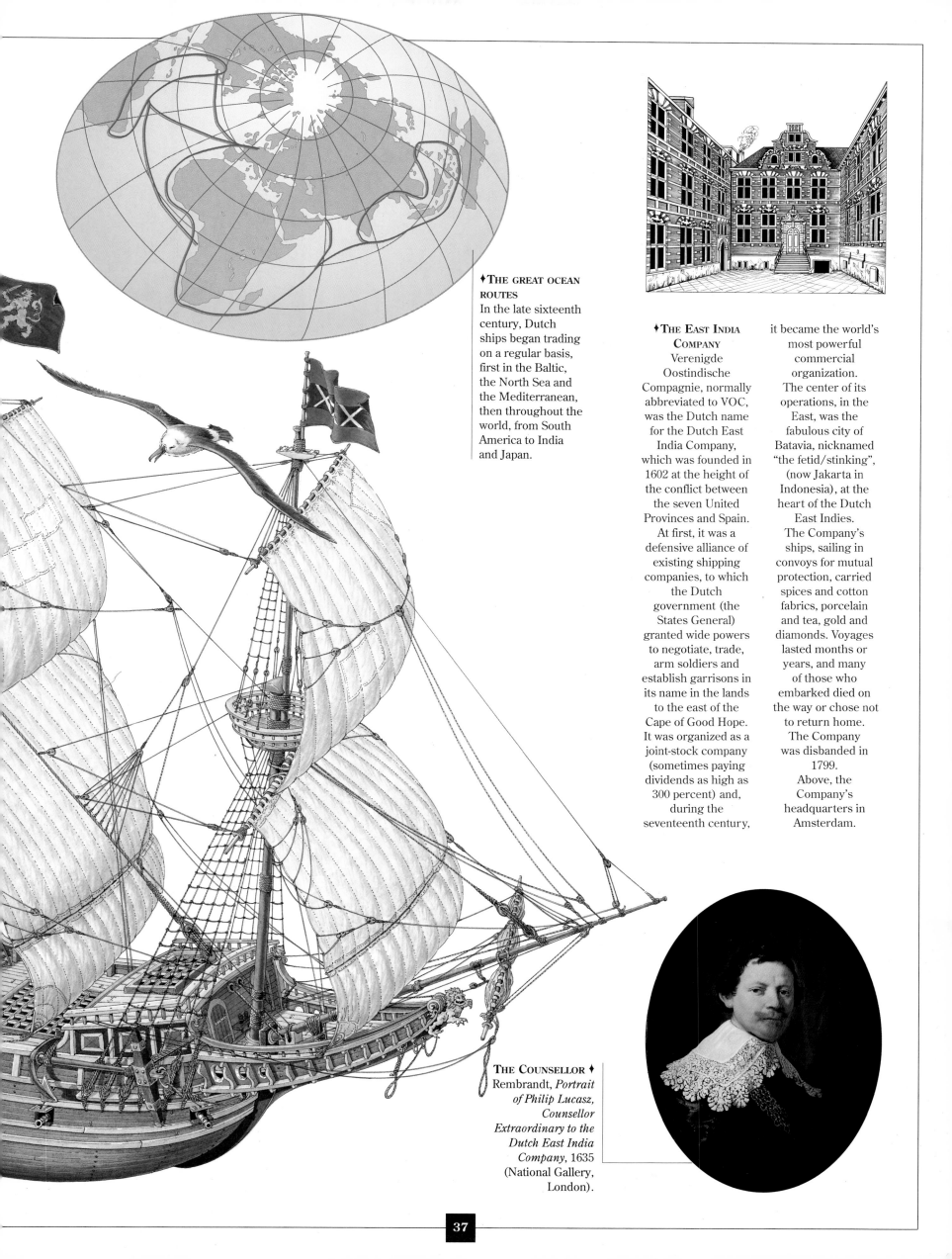

♦ THE GREAT OCEAN ROUTES
In the late sixteenth century, Dutch ships began trading on a regular basis, first in the Baltic, the North Sea and the Mediterranean, then throughout the world, from South America to India and Japan.

♦ THE EAST INDIA COMPANY
Verenigde Oostindische Compagnie, normally abbreviated to VOC, was the Dutch name for the Dutch East India Company, which was founded in 1602 at the height of the conflict between the seven United Provinces and Spain. At first, it was a defensive alliance of existing shipping companies, to which the Dutch government (the States General) granted wide powers to negotiate, trade, arm soldiers and establish garrisons in its name in the lands to the east of the Cape of Good Hope. It was organized as a joint-stock company (sometimes paying dividends as high as 300 percent) and, during the seventeenth century, it became the world's most powerful commercial organization. The center of its operations, in the East, was the fabulous city of Batavia, nicknamed "the fetid/stinking", (now Jakarta in Indonesia), at the heart of the Dutch East Indies. The Company's ships, sailing in convoys for mutual protection, carried spices and cotton fabrics, porcelain and tea, gold and diamonds. Voyages lasted months or years, and many of those who embarked died on the way or chose not to return home. The Company was disbanded in 1799.
Above, the Company's headquarters in Amsterdam.

THE COUNSELLOR ♦
Rembrandt, *Portrait of Philip Lucasz, Counsellor Extraordinary to the Dutch East India Company*, 1635 (National Gallery, London).

CARTOGRAPHY

A seventeenth-century European's idea of the shape of his or her country, and of the world, was very similar to our own. Already in those days quite accurate maps were widely available. Not surprisingly, these maps were more correct in their representation of better-known areas – for example, the hinterland of big cities and coastlines adjacent to major ports – than they were in showing features of distant and unexplored territories, such as the courses of the great Russian rivers or the icy wastes of the far north. However, as navigation developed (and with it the need for ever greater precision in planning voyages) and as advances were made in techniques of measurement and drawing, there was a constant improvement in the quality of maps. In the seventeenth century, Holland was the leading producer of maps and nautical charts. Cartography developed hand in hand with publishing and, thanks to such booksellers and publishers as Blaeu and Hondius, atlases were found in many homes.

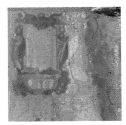

♦ MAPS AS DECOR
Maps were often displayed as part of the decoration and furnishings of homes in seventeenth-century Holland. They are seen used in this way in many paintings of interiors, such as Vermeer's *The Artist's Studio*, c.1665 (Kunsthistorisches Museum, Vienna), of which a detail is shown above.

♦ MAPS OF THE HEAVENS
As well as land maps and globes, Dutch cartographers produced maps of the night sky and planispheres. A celestial globe can be seen in the detail above from Vermeer's *The Astronomer*, 1668 (Louvre, Paris). A globe of this type constructed by Hondius in 1600 (left) is now kept at the Nederlands Historisch Scheepvaartsmuseum, Amsterdam.

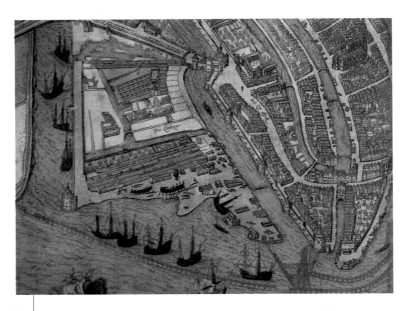

♦ THE DEVELOPMENT OF CARTOGRAPHY
In the forty-five years from 1572 to 1617, Georg Braun, a churchman of Cologne, and a cartographer called Frans Hogenberg completed a massive publishing project: *Civitates Orbis Terrarum*, or "Cities of the Earth". It was the first systematic attempt to represent the major cities of Europe, the African coast and the Near East. For the 531 plates that made up the work, Braun and Hogenberg relied on the collaboration of hundreds of cartographers, draftsmen, engravers, city authorities and individual citizens, who were invited to supply information and plans of their native city. The work was an enormous success: for the first time, travelers, navigators and merchants could refer to a guide illustrating the main buildings, fortifications, access routes and gates of each city. Information was also provided about the customs and dress of the inhabitants of each place.
Above, the plate of Amsterdam, 1572, from Volume I.

RYTHER'S ♦ THEODOLITE
Manufactured in 1590 by Augustine Ryther of London, this is one of the oldest known examples (Museo di Storia della Scienza, Florence).

SIGHTING SYSTEM ♦
Gun-type sights were replaced by a telescope in the eighteenth century.

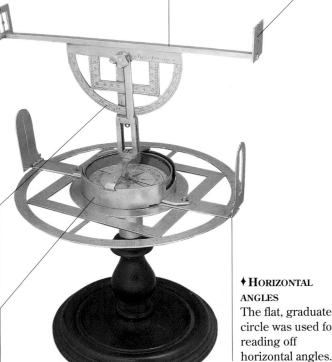

VERTICAL♦ ANGLES
Vertical angles were read off the graduated semi-circle.

A COMPASS ♦
A magnetic compass was incorporated into the theodolite.

♦ HORIZONTAL ANGLES
The flat, graduated circle was used for reading off horizontal angles.

♦ SCIENTIFIC INSTRUMENTS
The development of cartography in the seventeenth century would not have been possible without the progress that was also being made in the design of optical and measuring instruments. The theodolite was undoubtedly the most important new invention: it enabled the user to measure the angles between three different points on the ground. Then, if the length of one of the sides of the triangle was known, the lengths of the other two could be calculated.

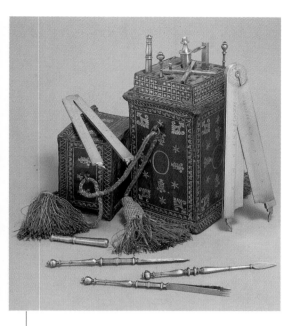

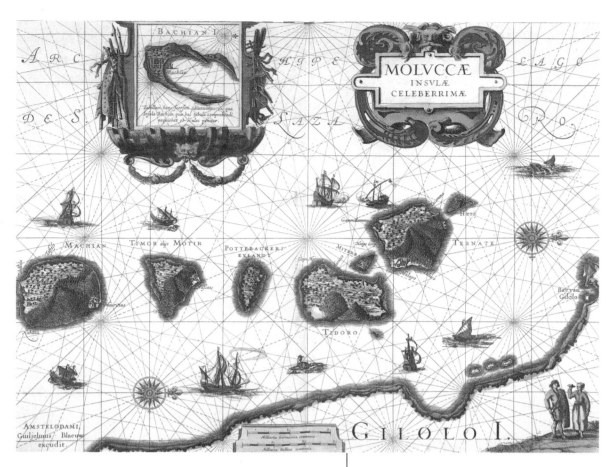

♦ MATHEMATICAL INSTRUMENTS
For conducting surveys in the field, a topographer would have used a number of instruments. The leather case shown above, containing measuring instruments, compasses, rulers and pencils, dates from the middle of the seventeenth century (Museo di Storia della Scienza, Florence).

♦ THE MOLUCCAS
In 1607 the Dutch took possession of the Moluccas, a group of spice islands in the Pacific Ocean. Reliable new maps were essential to sailors. One of the chief customers for such maps was, of course, the East India Company.

♦ THE GEOGRAPHER
Vermeer's famous painting, c.1668 (Städelsches Kunst-institut, Frankfurt), shows a man using compasses to measure distances on a map. On top of the cupboard is a globe, while a framed map hangs on the wall. It has been noticed that the features of the man's face occur in others of Vermeer's paintings and some scholars think they are those of the artist himself.

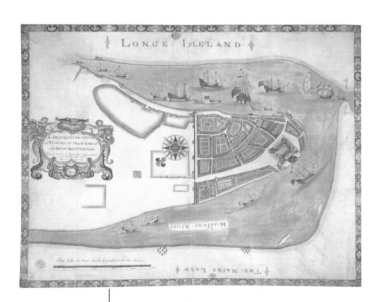

♦ MANHATTAN
In 1626, roughly a century after its discovery by Giovanni da Verrazano, the peninsula inhabited by the Manhattos, a tribe of Algonquin Indians, was bought by the Dutch for sixty guilders and became known as Nieuw Amsterdam. Soon people began to settle in the surrounding areas of Nieuw Haarlem and Breukelen. Pieter Stuyvesant was the governor from 1647 to 1664, when the town fell into the hands of the English and was renamed New York. This map of 1664, by an unknown author, (British Library, London) was presented to the Duke of York.

VERMEER

Jan Vermeer is the other outstanding Dutch painter of the seventeenth century. Whereas Rembrandt was prolific in his output, no more than thirty-five authenticated works by Vermeer have come down to us. He was little known in his lifetime and his cool, lucid scenes, charged with an atmosphere of silent suspense, remained unnoticed by scholars until the beginning of the twentieth century. Among those then to rediscover Vermeer's virtues was Marcel Proust.

♦VERMEER'S LIFE
Little is known of Vermeer's personality and career. On the other hand, we do have detailed information about his family's financial affairs and those of his parents. It is an all-too-familiar story of difficult circumstances, unpaid debts, broken promises, creditors, court cases and failed business ventures.

Jan Vermeer was born in Delft in 1632. His father was a textile worker, inn-keeper and, on occasion, art dealer. His son continued to run the inn and deal in pictures, but without much success. We know nothing of how he learned to paint, though at the age of twenty-one he was already enrolled in the artists' guild. In 1653, Jan was married to Catharina Bolnes, from a Catholic family and socially his superior.

♦THE GEOGRAPHER
A detail of the face of the girl portrayed in *The Artist's Studio* is shown at the top of this column. Above is *The Geographer*, c.1668 (Städelsches Kunstinstitut, Frankfurt).

♦THE MAP
Maps were hung, like paintings, in Dutch houses. The map in many of Vermeer's works has been interpreted as proof that he was pointing to the similarity between painters and cartographers, both descriptive artists.

♦THE CURTAIN
As in the theater, in Vermeer's dramatic scene, the curtain separates the spectator and the actors.

♦EVERYDAY OBJECTS
Careful examination of Vermeer's paintings enables us to reconstruct the furnishings and décor of his house.

Vermeer was a painter of interiors, or perhaps we should say of one interior, as the majority of his paintings are set in a single room, presumably in the artist's house. As the French writer Marcel Proust noted, all are "fragments of the same world". *The Artist's Studio, above, c.1665 (Kunsthistorisches Museum, Vienna), is the work most typical of this private world, haunted by recurrent objects and mysterious figures.*

♦ **WOMAN WITH A PEARL NECKLACE**
1662-1665 (Gemäldegalerie, Berlin). From Vermeer's paintings, we even know the contents of the family wardrobe. The yellow silk jacket edged with ermine which appears in this painting is precisely described in the inventory of belongings drawn up on the artist's death.

WOMAN READING ♦ A LETTER
1662-1665 (Rijksmuseum, Amsterdam). Reading and writing are frequently shown in Vermeer's paintings, enhancing the mysterious silence which seems to bathe his subjects. The familiar map again appears in this painting of a woman reading.

♦ **FINAL YEARS**
Vermeer took a Catholic wife and apparently had no compunction about abandoning his Calvinist beliefs. Two weeks after his engagement, he was married. Catharina bore him fifteen children, four of whom died in infancy, and his large family certainly did not make life any easier.

♦ **LADY AT THE VIRGINALS**
c.1670 (National Gallery, London). The Cupid in the painting on the wall holds a playing card: a symbol that love is governed by chance.

DELFT ♦
Jan Vermeer, *View of Delft*, 1658 (Mauritshuis, The Hague).

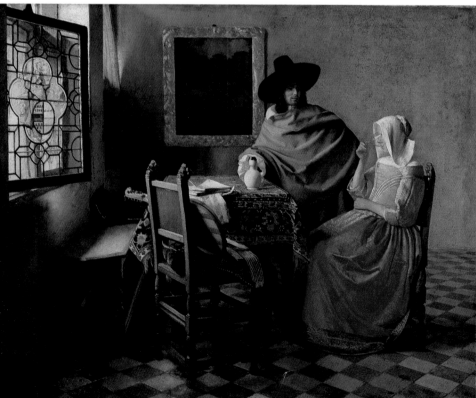

♦ **THE GLASS OF WINE**
c.1660 (Gemälde-galerie, Berlin). The perspective effects typical of Vermeer's works have led to the supposition that the artist used a fixed camera obscura when painting interiors like this. A detail is shown below.

His mother-in-law did all that she could to help them. However, in 1675, when he was only forty-three years old, Vermeer died. Most of his paintings were then sold to raise the money to pay off his debts.

Two years later, Catharina wrote these words concerning her husband's death: "Because the children were a great burden, and because we lacked financial means, he fell into such a depression and lethargy that he lost his health in the space of a day and a half, and died."

HOMES AND HOUSES

Simplicity and decorum characterized dress and domestic furnishings in Calvinist Holland. Seventeenth-century paintings give a very clear idea of how Dutch homes looked inside – with large wardrobes made of solid wood; the kitchen table invariably positioned close to the window – the main source of light – and sometimes covered with a piece of material or a rug; floors paved with large glazed or terra-cotta tiles; pictures on the walls; and a broad fireplace in the smoky kitchen. Outside, town houses were often crowned with a crow-stepped gable. Of course, there were considerable differences between the dwellings of rich and poor. Indeed, not everyone had a house: Amsterdam attracted any number of unemployed foreigners, who lived for longer or shorter periods without a roof over their heads. The more fortunate might live in a basement or a wooden lean-to leading to an internal courtyard. Those higher up the social scale might aspire to a modest house built on a single, narrow plot of ground, a comfortable "double dwelling", or possibly an aristocratic town residence.

♦ ROPE AND PULLEY ♦
A rope and pulley installed on the upper part of the façade were used for lifting goods and furniture to the floor on which they were needed.

NEW STYLE ♦
Bell-shaped gables came into fashion around 1660.

♦ REMBRANDT'S HOUSE
Rembrandt's house, on the part of the St Anthoniesbreestraat known as the Jodenbreestraat, was in the old Jewish district. Today it is a museum.

OLD STYLE ♦
The narrow façades of medieval buildings had simple triangular gables. Not until the sixteenth century did the characteristic stepped gables come into fashion.

♦ THE CANAL
Almost every house had access to one of the city's main waterways, and people would keep a boat moored near their home.

8. REMBRANDT'S LIFE STORY ♦ *In 1641, Saskia had a son, Titus. The next year she died, and was buried in the Oudekerk. A widow, Geertge Dircx joined the household as the child's nurse, and soon became Rembrandt's mistress. By 1649, relations between Rembrandt and Geertge had broken down, and she sued him for breach of promise of marriage. The court ordered Rembrandt to pay her an allowance of 200 guilders a year – evidently not enough for Geertge, for she also pawned jewelery that Rembrandt had given her and which had once belonged to Saskia. This led to Rembrandt's accusing her of dissolute behavior and having her locked up in a reformatory, although he continued to pay her allowance. Geertge was held for five years and died soon after her release. Meanwhile, Rembrandt formed a relationship with a country girl in his service: Hendrickje Stoffels. He did not marry her for, by remarrying, he would lose his entitlement to benefit from Saskia's will. Together, the couple indulged extravagant tastes, contracting one debt after another. ➤*

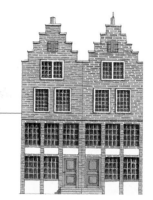

♦ WINDOWS
The windows on the middle stories usually had fixed panes at the top.

♦ HOIST
In addition to the rope and pulley, many houses had a hoist in the attic for lifting heavy loads.

THE ROOF ♦
The gable concealed a steeply pitched roof consisting of wooden timbers covered with the wavy-edged pantiles that are characteristic of Dutch houses.

♦ THE ATTIC
The attic rather than the cellar was used for storing many goods, as it was dry and less accessible to rats and mice.

♦ BEDROOMS
The bedrooms, furnished with large four-poster beds, were on the upper floors.

♦ LIVING ROOM
The entrance-way, main reception room and kitchens were on the raised ground floor.

♦ STAIRS
The floors were connected by a wooden spiral staircase, roughly in the middle of the house.

♦ THE KITCHEN
The kitchen was at the rear of the house, at ground-floor level.

♦ THE PANTRY
The pantry might be beneath or next to the kitchen.

♦ CELLAR AND STORE ROOM
Goods not needing a dry environment were stored in the cellars, below street level.

♦ FOUNDATIONS
Brick gradually replaced wood as a building material. Therefore, new buildings were heavier than in the past and stronger foundations were needed to support them. Hundreds of piles up to 11 meters (36 feet) long were sunk down through the surface layer of peat into the sandy soil below.

♦ CHANGING STYLES
Houses in the Middle Ages had simple triangular gables, but, as time went by, more elaborate styles became fashionable. Typical of the seventeenth century are bell-shaped gables and gables of which the central rectangular part was narrower than the façade itself.

In the Middle Ages, most houses in Holland were built of wood. A series of disastrous fires during the fifteenth century convinced the city authorities that they should ban wood as a building material, in favor of brick or, more rarely, stone. From 1452, side walls had to be built of brick. Wood was still permitted for façades up until 1669, when it was expressly forbidden by law. By that time, however, wood was generally being used only for the roof timbers.
When Amsterdam's old Town Hall burned down, Rembrandt, fascinated by ruins, made a drawing of it.

GENRE PAINTING AND INTERIORS

Paintings of scenes from daily life are sometimes described by art historians as genre paintings. They were particularly popular with the people of seventeenth-century Holland, whose tastes seemed to be satisfied most of all by paintings of interiors. The German art historian Max Friedländer wrote: "History painting is concerned with events that happened once, at a given time and place; genre painting with everyday life. Genre was particularly popular in the north, where the republican Dutch, within their narrow, victoriously defended borders, viewed their secure existence with a sense of satisfaction." What was it about interior paintings that so appealed to the Dutch? In these pictures they saw themselves: their houses, possessions and labors. The paintings mirrored their hard-won prosperity achieved by obedience to Biblical precepts. (Calvinism emphasized thrift and hard work as religious virtues.) The people in the paintings are anonymous and so anybody could identify him or herself with them. At the time, such an idea was extraordinary and repugnant to academic artists and art connoisseurs all over Europe, who were convinced that a painting worthy of the name should feature gods, heroes or saints. In their view, a scene of daily life reflected the tastes of the vulgar, uncultured bourgeoisie. Nevertheless, a considerable number of great artists subsequently devoted themselves to genre painting of this kind. For us today, genre paintings are works of beauty and a precious source of information about the social life of the past.

♦ FIREMAN'S NIGHTMARE
This curious illustration of firemen at a blazing house was engraved by Jan van der Heyden. He was both a genre painter and chief of the fire service.
The engraving comes from his *Brandspuitenboeck* ("Fire Engine Book"), 1690 (Historisch Museum, Amsterdam).

TAVERN SCENES ♦
The low prices fetched by genre paintings, together with fierce competition, led artists increasingly to specialize in certain subjects. Jan Steen (1626-1679), for example, painted taverns frequented by drinkers, gamblers and soldiers.

1. Jan Steen, *The Cabaret*, 1660-1670 (Mauritshuis, The Hague).
2. Jan Steen, *The Prince's Birthday*, 1660-1670 (Rijksmuseum, Amsterdam).

DAILY LIFE ♦
1. Pieter de Hoogh, *The Linen Cupboard*, 1663 (Rijksmuseum, Amsterdam).
2. Adriaen van Ostade, *Peasant Gathering*, detail, 1661 (Rijksmuseum, Amsterdam).
3. Pieter de Hoogh, *Courtyard of a House in Delft*, 1658 (Noortman Gallery, London).
4. Frans van Mieris, *Two Old People at Table*, 1655-1660 (Uffizi, Florence).

CHURCHES ♦
Several genre painters found inspiration in the sober architecture of Dutch Protestant churches (and also in Catholic churches and synagogues). Two such artists were Emanuel de Witte (c.1617-1692) and Pieter Saenredam (c.1595-1665).
1. Pieter Saenredam, *Interior of St Lawrence Church, Alkmaar*, 1661 (Boymans, Rotterdam).
2. Emanuel de Witte, *Church Interior*, 1617-1622 (Musée Jeanne d'Aboville, La Fere).
3. Pieter Saenredam, *Interior of the Church of St Bavo, Haarlem*, 1635 (Rijksmuseum, Amsterdam).

2

3

4

3

THE REMBRANDT FAMILY

Rembrandt's distinctly non-conformist attitude to marriage sheds light on his idea of himself and his relationship with the society around him. It is clear that he could not stand rules and regulations, whether imposed by the church or by the civil authorities. He may have taken the view that his status as an artist exempted him from the standards of behavior expected of ordinary citizens. The fact is that Rembrandt chose to engage in at least two lengthy extra-marital relationships, and because of this generally earned the moral disapproval of society. He was also censured for his casual attitude to money. His extravagance in buying paintings, furniture and all kinds of collectors' items was the very opposite of the virtue of thrift, which was so important in the Calvinist view; and it was made worse by his failure to settle his debts. Eventually his assets had to be sold at auction.

♦ REMBRANDT'S MOTHER
Rembrandt's Mother, 1631 (Rijksmuseum, Amsterdam). Cornelia Willemsdr van Zuytbroeck was probably the model for the elderly women in her son's early works.

♦ REMBRANDT'S FATHER
Rembrandt's Father, 1630-31 (Mauritshuis, The Hague). Harmen Gerritsz van Rijn was a well-off Leiden miller, who had converted from Catholicism to Calvinism. He married Cornelia in 1589 and they had nine children.

SASKIA ♦
Saskia in Arcadian Costume, 1635 (National Gallery, London). Rembrandt and Saskia were married in 1634. They had one son, Titus, born in 1641. Saskia died in 1642.

HENDRICKJE ♦
Hendrickje Stoffels lived with Rembrandt from around 1648 until her death in 1663. This *Portrait of Hendrickje* was painted around 1654 (Louvre, Paris).

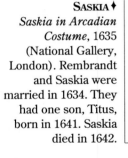

9. REMBRANDT'S LIFE STORY ♦ *In 1654, Rembrandt and Hendrickje chose not to appear when summoned before the church courts to answer a charge of concubinage (living together without being married). Hendrickje was later summoned alone, and instructed to repent. A daughter, Cornelia, was born the same year. Rembrandt sold few paintings and his debts mounted up. He tried to have the house registered as the property of his son Titus, to put it out of the grasp of his creditors, but to no avail: the move was illegal. Bankruptcy could not be avoided. In July 1656, an inventory was made of the goods kept in his house on the St Anthoniesbreestraat: 363 items including works of art, furniture, theatrical costumes and books. Titus (already registered as the beneficiary of his mother's estate) made a will in favor of Hendrickje and Cornelia, but granting his father the enjoyment of the property during his lifetime. However, this could not prevent Rembrandt's possessions being auctioned in 1657 and 1658. ⟫*

♦ SASKIA
Rembrandt, *Saskia* or *Bust of a Lady in a Cap Plumed with an Ostrich Feather*, c.1640 (Musée Bonnat, Bayonne).

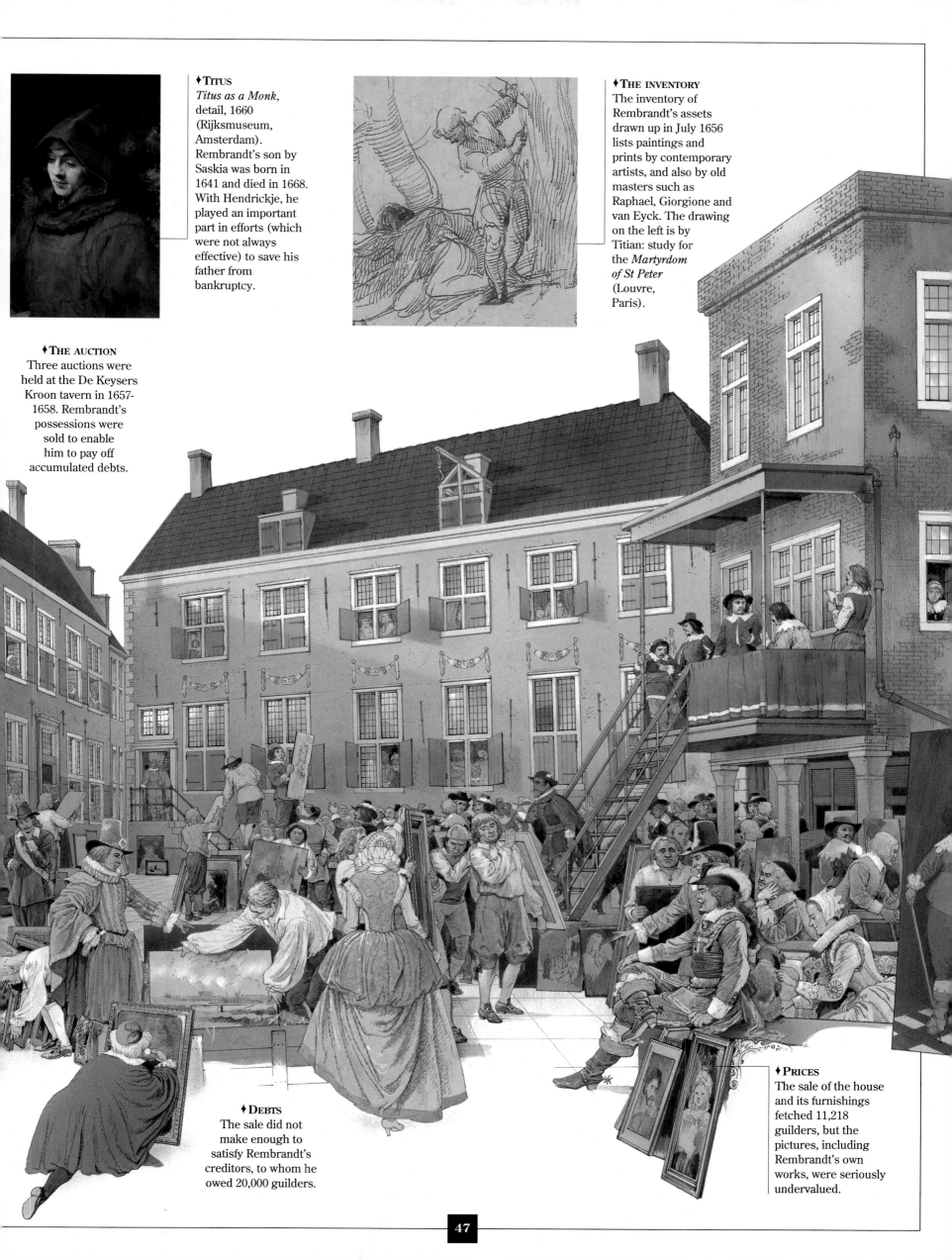

♦ TITUS
Titus as a Monk,
detail, 1660
(Rijksmuseum,
Amsterdam).
Rembrandt's son by
Saskia was born in
1641 and died in 1668.
With Hendrickje, he
played an important
part in efforts (which
were not always
effective) to save his
father from
bankruptcy.

♦ THE INVENTORY
The inventory of
Rembrandt's assets
drawn up in July 1656
lists paintings and
prints by contemporary
artists, and also by old
masters such as
Raphael, Giorgione and
van Eyck. The drawing
on the left is by
Titian: study for
the *Martyrdom
of St Peter*
(Louvre,
Paris).

♦ THE AUCTION
Three auctions were
held at the De Keysers
Kroon tavern in 1657-
1658. Rembrandt's
possessions were
sold to enable
him to pay off
accumulated debts.

♦ DEBTS
The sale did not
make enough to
satisfy Rembrandt's
creditors, to whom he
owed 20,000 guilders.

♦ PRICES
The sale of the house
and its furnishings
fetched 11,218
guilders, but the
pictures, including
Rembrandt's own
works, were seriously
undervalued.

THE WORKSHOP

Rembrandt's workshop, like that of other well-known Dutch artists of the period, served as a school as well as a production studio. Pupils came to him around the age of fifteen, many from other towns and cities. They all lived, worked, studied and slept in the workshop. Contracts that have survived reveal that Rembrandt charged the parents or guardians of his pupils a high fee for their teaching, board and lodging: it was not everyone who could afford to train with a painter held in such high regard. Works produced by pupils later on in their training in the workshop were sold by the master, who would often sign them with his own name. The master's word was law: he laid down the style, subject matter and price of his pupils' paintings, running the workshop to all intents and purposes as a business enterprise.

♦THE PAINTER'S STUDIO
Rembrandt, engraving, c.1648 (Louvre, Paris).

LIGHTING ♦
Large windows were essential to give a studio plenty of natural light.

MASTER AND PUPILS ♦
Many sketches and finished drawings provide information about the atmosphere of Rembrandt's studio. Master and pupils would generally work together on the same subject, all seated on stools around the model.

10. REMBRANDT'S LIFE STORY ♦ *In 1660, the poet Jeremias de Decker published* De Hollantsche Parnas, *a poem comparing Rembrandt to the ancient Greek painter Apelles. And Guercino, one of the finest Italian painters of the time, having seen some of Rembrandt's engravings, referred to him as "a great virtuoso". Meanwhile, the artist signed a contract with Titus and Hendrickje, giving them the exclusive right to market all works produced by himself (and his workshop) until seven years after his death. In exchange, they guaranteed him free board and lodging. The reasons for the agreement are clear: it enabled Titus and Hendrickje – who for some time had been conducting an art business of their own – to be first in line among Rembrandt's creditors, with a prior claim over any other parties. It left Rembrandt to get on with his work in peace. Even so, the family had to leave the large house and workshop on the St Anthoniesbreestraat for a more modest dwelling by the Rozengracht, in the working-class Jordaan district.* ➮

✦ DRAPERY
A studio would have a supply of materials of various kinds, which could be hung or draped over a frame or dummy for the pupils to copy.

✦ MODELS
It was normal practice to draw from life, often from nude models. Usually the models were from the lower classes, but often friends, relations or the pupils themselves would stand in.

✦ SCREENS
A series of screens enabled the master or pupils to work in isolation if they particularly needed to concentrate.

✦ STUDY MATERIALS
Rembrandt's passion for costumes and curiosities explains the presence in his studio of statues, armor and strange headgear.

✦ PAINTS
Rembrandt took great care in preparing his paints, often using new and expensive pigments, which were ground with a stone pestle.

♦THE WORK
Canvas, 363 x 438 cm
(143 x 172½ in),
1642 (Rijksmuseum,
Amsterdam).
The Night Watch,
possibly Rembrandt's
most famous
painting, was
commissioned in
1638 to mark the visit
to Amsterdam of the
French queen, Marie
de Médicis.

THE NIGHT WATCH

This painting represents the musketeers of the
Amsterdam Civic Guard with their captain, Frans
Banning Cocq. The names of eighteen of the people
portrayed are known. Only in the eighteenth century
did the work come to be called *The Night Watch*. It is a
misnomer because Rembrandt in fact painted the scene
taking place in daylight. The name has stuck.

♦THE CAPTAIN
Frans Banning Cocq
(1605-1655) was a
son-in-law of the
mayor of Amsterdam.
A wealthy and
ambitious magistrate,
he set great store
by his military rank:
the citizen militias
had played an
important part in
the war against
Spain.

To celebrate the
event, a number of
artists were
commissioned to
paint group portraits
of Amsterdam's
militia companies. For
his work, Rembrandt
received the high fee
of 1600 guilders.

The Night Watch *was a
group portrait, a genre
much favored at the time
in Holland. Generally,
subjects were shown
standing in a row or
arranged around a table.
Rembrandt, however,*

*created a natural, animated
scene, using lighting,
color and atmospheric
depth to extraordinary
effect. Many anonymous
bystanders are included,
as well as the eighteen
known portraits.*

♦A SELF-PORTRAIT?
At the back, a
partly hidden
face is peering over
the shoulder of the
man holding a
flag – possibly
representing
Rembrandt
himself.

♦ THE MUSKET
One of the keys to the picture is the militia company's pride and joy: the musket. A soldier on the left is loading his weapon; one in the center is firing; a third, to the right, is blowing into the chamber after discharging his piece.

♦ VIRTUOSO USE OF COLOR
Subtle modulations of light and tone create a "dense" atmosphere; skillful perspective has been used to foreshorten a lance; but most of all, Rembrandt's use of color has given extraordinary light and shade effects.

♦ "PLAYING CARDS BY COMPARISON"
After the size of the painting had been cut down (see right), the picture still included twenty-eight men, three children and a dog. The names of eighteen of the characters portrayed are included on the large shield above the corner of the archway in the background, which was added after Rembrandt's death. These eighteen had all paid a contribution to the fee that Rembrandt received for the painting. Those closer to the front paid more. The painting was immediately famous. One of Rembrandt's pupils, Samuel van Hoogstraten, wrote: "This work will outshine all its rivals. It is conceived with such painterly insight, so full of dramatic movement and so powerfully executed that similar paintings seem like playing cards by comparison."

♦ A DAYLIGHT SCENE
The painting was intended to hang in the Kloveniersdoelen, headquarters of the Amsterdam musketeers *(kloveniers)*. In 1715, however, the work was removed from there and trimmed down so that it could be hung in a smaller room in the town hall. The watercolor shown above, from a book by Jacob Cats, (kept in the Rijksmuseum, Amsterdam, with other seventeenth- and eighteenth- century copies) shows what Rembrandt's painting looked like originally. It also decides another issue, confirming the fact that *The Night Watch* was originally set in daylight. Grime settling on the canvas and possibly the changed role of the civic guard (they became night-time security patrols) may have created the impression that it was a night scene and so led to the wide use of its inappropriate title.

ETCHING

Making multiple copies of a single picture lowers costs and prices: a fact which did not escape the shrewd, business-minded artists of seventeenth-century Holland. They became expert in the technique of etching, which enabled them to make large numbers of prints of one original subject. These prints could then be widely distributed and served to publicize the artist's work. Prints were relatively cheap and so they found their way into almost every Dutch home. They tended to be the preferred medium for subjects with obvious popular appeal, such as calenders, caricatures, traditional stories, and so on. From producing prints, it was only a short step to producing illustrated periodicals, forerunners of the modern newspaper.

♦WOODCUT
Woodcut, the oldest technique for reproducing an image, was first practiced in Europe in the fourteenth century. The artist cuts into a block of soft wood (the matrix), leaving his design in relief. The design is then inked and printed onto paper.

♦ENGRAVING
Engravings made their appearance towards the end of the fifteenth century. The design is cut into a metal matrix, almost always made of copper. The plate may be line-engraved with a burin, or "drawn on with a steel needle" (the dry-point technique); or the image may be etched onto the plate by the action of acids (etching). In each case, the ink lies in the grooves cut into the plate and considerable pressure is needed to transfer it to paper.

♦ALBRECHT DÜRER
(1471-1528) The great German artist Dürer learned the rudiments of engraving from his father, who was a goldsmith. He became highly skilled in making woodcuts and line-engravings. Above, *Portrait of Willibald Pirkheimer*, woodcut, 1524.

4. BLACKENING ♦
The surface intended to take the drawing is smoked over a flame until it becomes an intense, even black. The preparatory stage is now complete.

1. THE PLATE ♦
Usually of copper, the plate is one or two millimeters (3-7 hundredths of an inch) thick and must have a mirror-smooth surface.

2. PREPARATION ♦
The edges of the plate are filed smooth to stop them cutting the paper. The surface is cleaned in a chalk solution, after which hand contact is avoided.

5. DRAWING ♦
The artist may draw directly onto the waxed ground. However, the more common method is to go over a drawing already done on tracing paper. In either case, the artist uses a steel needle, which delicately cuts into the wax to expose the metal plate beneath.

12. CHECKING ♦
The first proof is completed and the artist examines the result. Usually the stages of producing an etching are repeated several times. The plate is waxed again, a modified version of the drawing is done, and the plate immersed once more, until a satisfactory end result is achieved. Then printing begins in earnest. One plate may be used to make scores of copies, each of which is signed and numbered by the artist.

♦3. WAXING
A brush is used to spread a thin layer of liquid wax on both sides of the plate.

6. ACID ♦
The plate is immersed in a corrosive acid solution which attacks only those parts of the plate that are not protected by the wax, that is the parts exposed by the action of the needle. A few minutes' immersion is sufficient to etch the drawing onto the plate.

10. THE PRESS ✦
The plate is placed on the bed, which moves on gears between two rollers.

A sheet of moistened paper is laid gently on the plate and covered with a felt blanket.

✦11. PRINTING
When the spider wheel is turned, the entire sandwich of bed, plate, paper and blanket passes between the two rollers. Under intense pressure, the damp paper is forced into the etched grooves and absorbs the ink.

REMBRANDT ✦ AS AN ETCHER
The seventeenth century was the great age of print-making in Europe. Against this background, Rembrandt stands out as one of the finest etchers of all time, able to exploit all the expressive possibilities of the medium. Two examples of his work are shown here: above, *Windmill*, 1641, and below, *Faust*, c.1652 (Rijksmuseum, Amsterdam).

✦8. INKING
After the wax has been removed using turpentine, the plate is carefully cleaned, and then inked with a roller. This is done over a special stove: heating the plate ensures that the ink penetrates right into the etched lines.

✦9. CLEANING
The plate is wiped with a linen cloth, so that ink remains only in the etched grooves.

7. WASHING ✦
The plate is washed in water to remove all traces of acid.

11. REMBRANDT'S LIFE STORY ✦ *Hendrickje fell ill and in 1661 made a will bequeathing her property to Cornelia and, in the event of the child's death, to Titus. Rembrandt was appointed Cornelia's guardian and granted the enjoyment of her estate during his lifetime. This was intended to secure the inheritance against the claims of creditors. In the same year, Rembrandt painted* The Conspiracy of Claudius Civilis *for Amsterdam Town Hall (his former pupil Govaert Flinck was also involved in this project). The work shows an episode in the resistance of the Batavians (supposed ancestors of the Dutch) to Roman invaders. In 1663, for reasons which remain obscure, the picture was removed and returned to Rembrandt. Despite such tribulations, the artist was still admired and his etchings continued to be bought by the general public.* ⯈➤

SELF-PORTRAITS

Seventeenth-century artists painted many self-portraits, sometimes including symbols of their profession. Below is Rembrandt's *Self-portrait, with Palette, Brushes and Maulstick* (a stick used to steady the hand holding the brush). He is dressed in working clothes. The two circles on the wall behind him have been interpreted in various ways, as secret signs, symbols of the perfection of God, a representation of the circular world maps which many people at this time had hanging on their walls, or simply a compositional device.

♦THE WORK
Canvas, 114.3 x 94 cm (45 x 37 in) (Kenwood House, London). The work is neither signed nor dated, but is believed to have been painted around 1665. This is based on a judgement of how old Rembrandt looks in the portrait, especially in comparison with his final self-portraits, in which he appears considerably more aged. The painting seems unfinished, with the turban only roughed in and the hands treated in sketchy fashion. The significance of the two circles behind the artist might also have been clearer, had the work been completed. Restoration work carried out fifty years ago revealed some damage to both the canvas and the picture surface, and X-rays showed that Rembrandt had repainted certain areas.

♦TWO ETCHINGS
The prints reproduced above, 1629 (Rijksmuseum, Amsterdam), and at the top of the column, 1630 (Bibliothèque Nationale, Paris), show how Rembrandt also used self-portraits to make studies of different facial expressions.

FIRST KNOWN EXAMPLE ♦
This *Self-portrait*, c.1628 (Rijksmuseum, Amsterdam), is the earliest of those that have survived. All the indications are that it was done as a study of light and shade.

♦YOUTHFUL WORK
Self-portrait, c.1629 (Mauritshuis, The Hague), a highly polished work.

♦A LATE EXAMPLE
Dated 1662, this *Self-portrait* now hangs in the Uffizi, Florence.

Rembrandt painted self-portraits throughout his career, and about forty have survived. Studying them is one way of following the development of his style. The early examples are in the highly finished manner of the time, more polished and including a greater amount of detail than the later ones. Portraits from his maturity tend to be thickly loaded with paint, with a richly worked surface. And those of his final years are more sketchy, almost impressionistic, as is very evident in the canvas above.

ARTISTIC PRIDE ♦
Self-portrait at the Age of 34, 1640 (National Gallery, London). Apparently inspired by the works of Titian and Raphael, Rembrandt here painted himself dressed in sixteenth-century style. He seems to have wanted to put himself on a par with great artists of the past.

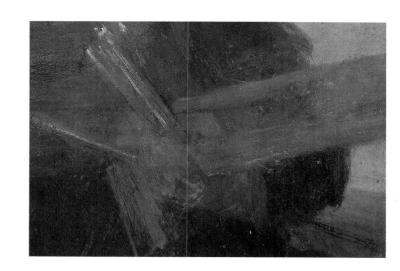

Most of Rembrandt's painting is characterized by the distinctive way in which he used paint as a material: not only to indicate the color of a surface but also to convey texture.

For this reason, Rembrandt was often accused of applying paint in a lumpy fashion. In fact, his work reveals that he was constantly experimenting with texture. His later works contain areas where the paint is very thinly applied. This is evident in the two details above: though unfinished, they illustrate how Rembrandt sought to suggest rather than represent reality.

AN "IMPROVED" ♦ SELF-PORTRAIT
Doubts as to who painted this portrait, and of whom, have surrounded this painting, which dates from 1639-1640 (Uffizi, Florence). X-ray examination suggests it may be a self-portrait, retouched to make the features less stern and forbidding.

♦ IN COSTUME
Self-portrait in Fancy Dress, 1635-1636 (Mauritshuis, The Hague). In many self-portraits Rembrandt is in costume. He and members of his family also appear in disguise in his paintings of mythological subjects, perhaps to avoid paying for models for these works.

♦ IN DISGUISE
The Prodigal Son, c.1635 (Gemäldegalerie, Dresden). This self-portrait of Rembrandt and Saskia in fancy dress is thought to represent the Bible story.

♦ IN ORIENTAL COSTUME
There is some doubt about the attribution of this *Self-portrait (or Portrait) of Rembrandt in Oriental Costume with Poodle*, c.1631 (Petit Palais, Paris).

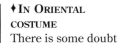

STILL LIFE

In seventeenth-century Holland, pictures were a form of merchandise and there was considerable consumer demand for them. The market was well supplied and there was sometimes over-production. In the case of pictures representing objects in everyday use, such as a bowl of fruit or a jug, purchasers wanted the subject to be depicted as realistically as possible. The artist would try to imitate reality to perfection, emphasizing the most agreeable and intriguing details. It was as if, in reproducing ornamental items, animals and flowers, the painter was competing with a craftsman, or with nature itself. The Dutch weakness for near-perfect imitations of reality explains the great success of still life at this time.

♦ **PLAY OF LIGHT**
Abraham van Beyeren (c.1620-1690) painted his still life subjects with all the analytical skill required by the genre and also excelled in showing the play of light on the objects. *Still Life with Crab and Fruit* (Mauritshuis, The Hague).

12. REMBRANDT'S LIFE STORY ♦ *In 1663, a terrible plague broke out in Amsterdam, killing some 1700 people. Among the victims was Hendrickje, whom Rembrandt managed to have buried in a rented tomb in the Westerkerk. Business was bad, and the painter had some difficulty paying the rent. Commissions were few and far between. But soon afterwards, probably in 1665, Rembrandt was asked to paint* The Jewish Bride, *and things improved when Titus succeeded in recovering a debt. Nothing daunted Rembrandt, as he continued to expand his collection of pictures, prints, shells and other items whenever he could.* ➤

TABLES ♦
Tables loaded with crockery, fruit, jugs of wine and similar household items were typical in particular of the Haarlem school of painters, of which Willem Claesz Heda and Pieter Claesz were the greatest representatives.
1. Willem Kalff, *Still Life*, c.1650 (Mauritshuis, The Hague).
2. Willem Claesz Heda, *Still Life*, 1634 (Boymans, Rotterdam).
3. Willem Claesz Heda, *Luncheon with Lobsters*, 1648 (Hermitage, St Petersburg).

ANIMALS ♦
The price of an ox in seventeenth-century Holland was 90 guilders. A painting of the subject (or indeed a portrait) could be had for between 25 and 60 guilders (provided that the painter was not a celebrity). Melchior Hondecoeter (1636-1695) was one of the best animal painters.

1. Melchior Hondecoeter, *Peacocks and Ducks*, 1680 (Wallace Collection, London).
2. Carel Fabritius, *The Goldfinch* (Mauritshuis, The Hague).

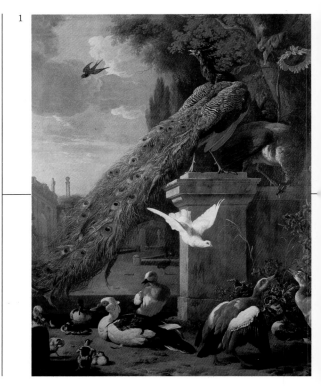

FLOWERS ♦
Since medieval times flowers had been symbols of rebirth, the Virgin Mary and beauty. In seventeenth-century Dutch painting a flower was just a flower: a challenge to the painter's virtuosity with paint.
1. Maria van Osterwyck, *Flowers, Fruit, Insects* (Palatine Gallery, Florence).
2. Ambrosius Bosschaert the Elder, *Vase of Flowers*, c.1620 (Mauritshuis, The Hague).

2

3

STUDIES OF ✦ A LEMON
The illustrations on the right are close-ups of the lemons from the three paintings on the left. Careful training and long experience were needed to achieve the technical skill for rendering detail realistically. However, few seventeenth-century Dutch genre painters were able to make a living by using this skill. Van Goyen had to supplement his income by dealing in tulips, van de Velde by managing a linen factory, and Steen by running an inn.

1

2
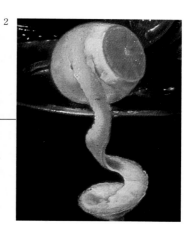

3

2

REMBRANDT ✦
Still life was not a genre much practiced by Rembrandt. One example from c.1639 is *Child and Dead Peacocks*, (Rijksmuseum, Amsterdam).

2

VANITAS ✦
A special kind of still life, which was popular throughout Europe, was the *Vanitas*. This type of painting, featuring skulls, hour-glasses, candles and faded flowers, was intended to remind the viewer of the fragility and fleetingness of human existence. Abraham van der Schoor, *Vanitas* (Rijksmuseum, Amsterdam).

THE JEWISH BRIDE

In portrait painting, it was not uncommon to cast the sitter in the role of a character from history or the Bible. In this double portrait, the reference is to a story in Genesis 26. Husband and wife, Isaac and Rebecca, pretend to be brother and sister, in order to deceive the Philistines, but are found out by King Abimelech. The true identity of the man and woman is unknown. Some think they are Rembrandt's son, Titus, and his wife.

♦ **THE WORK**
Canvas, 121.5 x 166.5 cm (48 x 65½ in) (Rijksmuseum, Amsterdam). It is possible to make out the artist's signature, but the work is undated. 1662-1664 seems likely.
The work did not become known as *The Jewish Bride* until the nineteenth century, when it was acquired, in 1825, by the English art dealer John Smith. Some believe the man and woman in the painting to be Rembrandt's son and daughter-in-law, Magdalena. There are various other theories (none very convincing), including that the painting is of the Jewish poet Miguel de Barrios and his wife Abigail de Pina, or even of the Persian king Cyrus and the shepherdess Aspasia, characters in a play by the poet Jacob Cats in 1656.

STUDY FOR ANOTHER BRIDE ♦
This pen drawing, c.1635 (Nasional Museet, Stockholm), is a preliminary study for Rembrandt's large etching *The Jewish Bride*.

♦ **TITUS AS A YOUNG MAN**
Rembrandt painted this *Portrait* of Titus around 1660 (Louvre, Paris). Here Titus looks considerably younger than the husband in *The Jewish Bride*, which was painted at about the same time. By this argument, it seems unlikely that the man Rembrandt portrayed in *The Jewish Bride* was Titus.

The Jewish Bride *is one of the paintings most characteristic of Rembrandt's late style. His life-long experimentation with paint had led him far from the tastes prevailing in the mid-seventeenth century, when the fashion throughout Europe was for highly polished, luminous paintings in the Baroque manner. Rembrandt was capable of upsetting his customers (who in some cases went so far as to refuse the paintings they had commissioned) by his employment of a rapid impasto technique. This involved laying on thick slabs and clots of paint and working them over the surface, often with the help of a palette knife.*
To experience their full effect, the paintings are best viewed from a distance, but few of Rembrandt's contemporaries were able to appreciate them.

THE WOMAN IN THE PAINTING? ♦
The sitter for this *Portrait of a Well-dressed Young Woman*, c.1665 (Museum of Fine Arts, Montreal), was quite probably Magdalena van Loo, the wife of Titus. On the other hand, some people believe the painting to be a portrait of Hendrickje Stoffels.

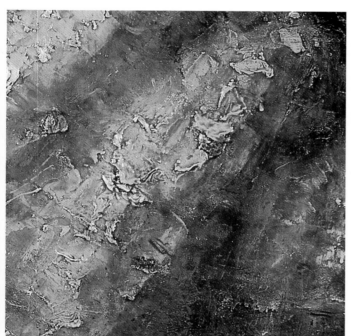

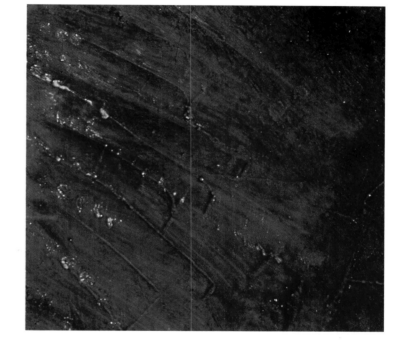

✦TWO COLORS
Rembrandt used variations of only two basic colors for his painting of *The Jewish Bride*: the green-gold of the bridegroom's garments – rich and full-bodied in the prominent sleeve, subdued in other areas – and the reddish-orange of the bride's dress, shot with delicate highlights in the bodice. The paint is laid on in lumps and flakes, reflecting the light to surprising effect. In this case, Rembrandt has used that technique of applying paint to suggest the texture of fabrics. In other works he applied the same technique successfully to make objects of every kind stand out and look real. Someone said of one of his portraits that it could be picked up by the nose of the sitter. Rembrandt's works have to be viewed from a distance. In fact, he would warn his customers not to approach too close, saying: "You would find the smell of the paint offensive." The paint, as Gérard de Lairesse (1641-1711) wrote disapprovingly, "runs all over the picture to form a dirty mess".

THE PUPILS

The young men who came to study with Rembrandt wanted to learn to paint like him. They were concerned to increase their chances of making painting a financially rewarding career for themselves. In this respect, Rembrandt's workshop was no different from any other school run by a well-known artist. Most of his pupils would already have completed an initial apprenticeship with another teacher before coming to him for a further period of study. In accordance with the rules of the painters' guild, the works the pupils produced during their time with him would be signed by the master and marketed as if they were his. This has led to works by Rembrandt's pupils being attributed to the master himself, and gives rise to changes of opinion about the attribution of paintings on the part of art critics. Only when his period of training was over could a pupil think of setting up a workshop on his own account.

♦ **MASTER AND PUPILS AT WORK**
This engraving of Rembrandt's workshop shows the master and his pupils practicing life drawing (Hessisches Landesmuseum, Darmstadt).

13. REMBRANDT'S LIFE STORY ♦ *On 29 December 1667, Rembrandt's workshop received a distinguished visitor: Grand Duke Cosimo III de' Medici, who was in Amsterdam with Filippo Corsini and had expressed a wish to see some works by "the famous painter". In 1668, Titus married Magdalena van Loo, but only a few months later he died. A daughter, Titia, was born in March 1669. In September of that year, Rembrandt painted* Simeon with the Infant Jesus, *which is possibly his last work. He died on 4 October 1669. Four days later he was buried in a rented tomb in Amsterdam's Westerkerk. Its exact location is not known. During the last months of his life, Rembrandt was all alone. Respectable society had never completely accepted certain of his attitudes; his painting no longer coincided with public taste. After his death, he was forgotten even by the critics.*

♦ **GERRIT DOU**
One of Rembrandt's first pupils, he joined the workshop from 1628 to 1631. Patient and meticulous, with a great concern for detail, he achieved success as a genre painter. Never departing from Rembrandt's earlier manner, he founded the Leiden school of highly polished painters.
The Charlatan, 1652 (Boymans, Rotterdam).

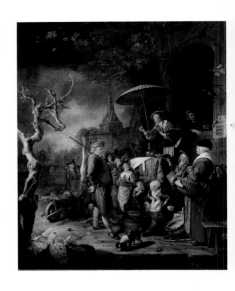

♦ **SAMUEL VAN HOOGSTRATEN**
(Dordrecht, 1627-1678). He went to study with Rembrandt in 1640 and then worked in London. He became a specialist in perspective.
Self-portrait, 1645 (Prince of Liechtenstein Collection, Vaduz).

♦ **GOVAERT FLINCK**
(Cleves, 1615 - Amsterdam, 1660). Flinck was a pupil in Rembrandt's workshop in 1633-1634. He later adopted a polished, classical style, and this won him many major public commissions. For a number of these he was in competition with Rembrandt.
Portrait of Rembrandt, c. 1633 (Gemäldegalerie, Berlin).

♦ **ISAAK JOUDERVILLE**
(Leiden, c.1612 - Amsterdam, 1645/1648). He was the orphan son of an inn-keeping family. His guardians apprenticed him to Rembrandt around 1629. In 1631-1632, he followed the master to Amsterdam, but later returned to Leiden. His imitation of Rembrandt's mannerisms shows clearly in his portraits.
Bust of Young Man, c.1631 (National Gallery of Ireland, Dublin).

♦ GERBRANDT VAN DEN EECKHOUT (Amsterdam, 1621 - 1674). He studied with Rembrandt from 1635 to 1640. His first love was for history painting, in which he combined the taste of Pieter Lastman with light and shadow effects learned from his master. Left: *The Prophet Elisha and the Shunammite Woman,* 1664 (Szépmüveszeti Museum, Budapest).

♦ JAN VICTORS (Amsterdam, 1619 - ?, c.1676). A strict Calvinist, he painted mainly biblical subjects, but did not achieve much success. Eventually he chose to go as a nursing auxiliary on an East India Company ship. He is thought to have died in the Far East. *Joseph Recounting his Dreams,* 1651 (Kunstmuseum, Düsseldorf).

♦ CAREL FABRITIUS (Midden-Beemster, 1624 - Delft, 1654). His master's *alter ego,* Fabritius worked closely with Rembrandt, especially as a portraitist. His clear, linear style of painting was an important influence on Jan Vermeer. *Portrait of Abraham de Potter,* c.1648 (Rijksmuseum, Amsterdam).

♦ FERDINAND BOL (Dordrecht, 1616 - Amsterdam, 1680). Rembrandt's pupil from c.1636 to 1642. He became an influential member of the artists' guild. His later style was lighter and more classical than that of his master. *Elisha Refusing Naaman's Gifts,* 1661 (Historisch Museum, Amsterdam).

♦ WILLEM DROST The only documented information we have about Drost's career is that he was in Venice in the mid-seventeenth century, following a period of apprenticeship with Rembrandt. Some works once believed to be by Rembrandt have recently been attributed to Drost. *Daniel's Vision,* 1650-1652 (Gemäldegalerie, Berlin).

♦ NICOLAES MAES (Dordrecht, 1634 - Amsterdam, 1693). Maes was one of Rembrandt's most successful pupils. He began as a history painter, switched to genre, and finally devoted himself to portrait painting, adopting a fashionable style which was inspired by Flemish Baroque, as shown here. *Portrait of Jacob Trip,* 1659-1660 (Mauritshuis, The Hague).

♦ BARENT FABRITIUS (Midden-Beemster, 1622 - Amsterdam, 1673). The younger brother of Carel, and greatly influenced by him, Fabritius worked closely with patrons in Leiden. There is no proof that he was part of Rembrandt's workshop. Portraiture and history painting were his interests. *Peter in the House of Cornelius,* detail, 1653 (Duke Anton Ulrich Museum, Brunswick).

◆ KEY DATES IN REMBRANDT'S LIFE

1606 Rembrandt Harmenszoon van Rijn born on 15 July in Leiden, Holland. His father owns a mill on the river Rhine.

1609 The seven provinces of the northern Netherlands sign a twelve-year truce with Spain, having first declared their independence from Spanish rule in 1579.

1621 Rembrandt becomes a pupil in the workshop of Jacob van Swanenburgh, a local painter, who teaches him the basic techniques of drawing and perspective.

1624 Ready to continue his studies with a master of greater talent, Rembrandt goes to Amsterdam to join the school of Pieter Lastman. After six months, he returns to Leiden and opens a workshop in partnership with another young painter, Jan Lievens.

1625 Frederick Henry, Prince of Orange, is appointed Stadholder of the United Provinces.

1626 On payment of 60 guilders, the Dutch West India Company acquires a peninsula in North America inhabited by the Manhattan Indians. They found the city of Nieuw Amsterdam, later renamed New York.

1628 Rembrandt and Lievens are joined by their first pupil, the fifteen-year-old Gerrit Dou, an indication of the growing importance of their workshop.

1630 Rembrandt and Lievens come to the attention of Constantijn Huygens, Secretary to the Stadholder.

1631 Rembrandt goes to live in Amsterdam and joins the household of art dealer Hendrick van Uylenburgh. Here he meets Hendrick's niece Saskia, wealthy daughter of a well-known magistrate.

1632 In January, Rembrandt paints *The Anatomy Lesson of Dr Tulp*, his first prestigious commission since arriving in Amsterdam. Birth, in Holland, of Baruch Spinoza, one of the greatest philosophers of the period.

1634 Rembrandt marries Saskia, thereby gaining wealth and social advancement. The Stadholder Frederick Henry asks him to do a series of paintings of Christ's Passion.

1639 Rembrandt and Saskia move to a large house on the St Anthoniesbreestraat, where Rembrandt installs his impressive art collection.

1642 Saskia, having recently given birth to a son, dies on 14 June. Rembrandt takes on Geertge Dircx, to help him rear the infant Titus. She becomes Rembrandt's mistress.

1648 Philip IV of Spain signs a peace treaty with the United Provinces at Münster, recognizing their sovereignty after more than seventy years of conflict.

1651 By the Navigation Act, the England of Oliver Cromwell assumes a monopoly of colonial trade, closing its empire to foreign ships. Seriously damaged by this measure, the United Provinces go to war with Britain.

1656 Rembrandt's financial situation, already precarious, is aggravated by the crisis brought on by the war. Creditors are no longer prepared to bear with his huge debts. The authorities draw up an inventory of his possessions and his art collection is disposed of at three public auction sales held in 1657-1658.

1663 Plague breaks out in Amsterdam. One of the victims is Hendrickje Stoffels, Rembrandt's companion since 1648 and mother of their daughter Cornelia.

1667 Rembrandt is visited in his workshop by Cosimo III de' Medici. In Amsterdam on business, the Grand Duke of Tuscany has expressed a wish to see works by the famous artist.

1669 Rembrandt dies and is buried in an anonymous rented tomb in Amsterdam's Westerkerk.

◆ WHERE TO SEE WORKS BY REMBRANDT

Rembrandt was a prolific artist and his works have found their way to museums all over the world, from his native Holland to France, the United States and Russia. Listed below are museums which have significant collections of paintings by Rembrandt. We have not included private collections, or museums which own only a few of his works.

HOLLAND

RIJKSMUSEUM, AMSTERDAM
Rembrandt's most famous painting, known as *The Night Watch* (1642), hangs in this museum, which also owns some of his best-known portraits (*Portrait of Haesje van Cleyburg*, 1634; *Portrait of Maria Trip*, c.1639; *The Painter's Mother as the Prophetess Anna*, 1631; *The Physician Ephraim Bueno*, c.1647; *Titus as a Monk*, 1660), self-portraits (*Self-portrait*, c.1628, and *Self-portrait as the Apostle Paul*, 1661), and biblical episodes (*Joseph Recounting his Dreams*, c.1633, and *Anna and Tobit*, 1626).

MAURITSHUIS, THE HAGUE
The Mauritshuis houses fifteen or so works by Rembrandt, including a portrait of an old man – probably the artist's father – and three self-portraits, one of which cannot be attributed with absolute certainty. The real gem of this collection is *The Anatomy Lesson of Dr Nicolaes Tulp*, the work Rembrandt painted in Amsterdam in early 1632, shortly after his arrival in the city.

FRANCE

LOUVRE, PARIS
The Louvre galleries are home to ten or so of Rembrandt's works, including *The Supper at Emmaus* (1648), four self-portraits and portraits of his companion Hendrickje Stoffels and his son Titus, painted in 1645 and 1660 respectively.

GERMANY

GEMÄLDEGALERIE, BERLIN
This museum owns a further two self-portraits, dating from around 1633 and 1634. Also on show are canvases of episodes from both Old and New Testaments: *Bathsheba at her Toilet with David's Letter* (1654), *Tobit Accusing Anna of Stealing a Kid* (1645), *The Parable of the Rich Fool* (1627) and *Christ and the Samaritan Woman at the Well* (1659).

ALTE PINAKOTHEK, MUNICH
Eleven works by Rembrandt are kept here, nine of them representing biblical episodes. Some belong to the Passion series commissioned by the Stadholder Frederick Henry of Orange through his Secretary Constantijn Huygens: *Adoration of the Shepherds* (1646), *Erection of the Cross* (c.1634), *Entombment* (c.1635-39), *Resurrection* (c.1635-39) and *Ascension* (1636).

ENGLAND

NATIONAL GALLERY, LONDON
Among the works by Rembrandt at the National Gallery, the best known are a *Self-portrait at the Age of 34* (1640), a portrait of *Saskia in Arcadian Costume* (1635), *Woman Bathing in a Stream* (1645), a portrait of Hendrickje Stoffels dating from around 1656 and an *Adoration of the Shepherds* (1646). The latter is a variant of the work painted in the same year for Prince Frederick Henry of Orange.

RUSSIA

HERMITAGE, ST PETERSBURG
Of the sixteen paintings by Rembrandt kept at the Hermitage, special mention should be made of *The Angel Preventing Abraham from Sacrificing Isaac* (1635), *Danae* (c.1642-43), *Holy Family* (1645), *Portrait of Man at a Writing Desk* (1631), *Saskia as Flora* (1634) and *Return of the Prodigal Son* (probably painted between 1662 and 1664).

UNITED STATES

METROPOLITAN MUSEUM OF ART, NEW YORK
The Metropolitan has a score of works by Rembrandt. They include a self-portrait dating from 1660, showing the artist with palette and brushes in hand; a painting of *Christ and the Samaritan Woman at the Well* (c.1659), closely related to the work on the same subject kept in Berlin; two portraits of Hendrickje, one (c.1656) depicting her as Flora; and a *Portrait of a Seated Woman* (1633).

NATIONAL GALLERY OF ART, WASHINGTON
Thirteen works by Rembrandt are kept in this museum, including eight portraits and one self-portrait. Painted in 1659, there is something unusual about this work: apart from the self-portrait belonging to the Wallraf-Richartz Museum in Cologne, it is the only one showing the painter with his body facing left.

(Works reproduced in their entirety are indicated with the letter E; those of which only a detail is featured are followed by the letter D).

The works reproduced in this book are listed here, with their date (when known), the place they are currently housed, and the page number. The numbers in bold type refer to the credits on page 64. Abbreviations: BMR, Boymans-van Beuningen Museum, Rotterdam; HMA, Historisch Museum, Amsterdam; KMV, Kunsthistorisches Museum, Vienna; RA, Rijksmuseum, Amsterdam.

ANONYMOUS
1 *The Anatomy Theatre at Leiden University*, 1644, engraving from *Atlas* by Frederick Müller (Bibliothèque Nationale, Paris) 35 E; **2** *Anna and Tobit*, engraving of a work by Marten van Heemskerck (Rijksprentenkabinett, Amsterdam) 21 E; **3** *Map of Manhattan*, 1664 (British Library, London) 39 E; **4** *The Netherlands in the Form of a Lion*, print inspired by an engraving by Pieter van der Keere, eighteenth century (University Library, Amsterdam); **5** *The Synod of Dort* (Historisch Museum, Rotterdam) 28 E; **6** *William III of Orange and his Predecessors*, engraving, 1672 (Historisch Museum, Rotterdam) 28 T
AVERCAMP, HENDRICK
7 *Winter Scene*, c.1608 (RA) 33 D
BERCKHEYDE, JOB ADRIAENSZ
8 *The Amsterdam Stock Exchange*, c. 1668 (BMR) 14 D
BEYEREN, ABRAHAM VAN
9 *Still Life with Crab and Fruit* (Mauritshuis, The Hague) 56 E
BOL, FERDINAND
10 *Allegory of the Admiralty*, c.1660 (HMA) 18 D; **11** *The Courage of Fabricius in the Camp of Pyrrhus*, 1650 (HMA) 19 E; **12** *Elisha Refusing Namaan's Gifts*, 1661 (HMA) 61 E; **13** *The Officers of the Wine Merchants' Guild*, c.1640-50 (Alte Pinakothek, Munich) 25 E; **14** *Portrait of Elisabeth Bas* (attr.), c.1640 (RA) 25 E; **15** *The Regents of the Leprosarium* (HMA) 29 E
BOSCH, HIERONYMOUS
16 *Hermits' Triptych*, 1510 (Doge's Palace, Venice) 7 D
BOSSCHAERT THE ELDER, AMBROSIUS
17 *Vase of Flowers*, c.1620 (Mauritshuis, The Hague) 57 E
BRUEGEL THE ELDER, PIETER
18 *Huntsmen in the Snow*, 1565 (KMV) 7 D
CANALETTO, BYNAME OF ANTONIO CANAL
19 *The Campo Santi Apostoli*, 1731-35 (private collection) 30 E
CATS, JACOB
20 *The Night Watch*, copied from Rembrandt's work, 1779 (RA) 51 E
DOU, GERRIT
21 *Anna and Tobit in his Blindness*, c.1630 (National Gallery, London) 21 E; **22** *The Charlatan*, 1652 (BMR) 60 E
DROST, WILLEM
23 *Daniel's Vision*, 1650-52 (Gemäldegalerie, Berlin) 61 E and D
DÜRER, ALBRECHT
24 *Portrait of Willibald Pirkheimer*, woodcut, 1524 52 E
DYCK, ANTHONY VAN
25 *Portrait of a Man and his Son*, 1628-29 (Louvre, Paris) 27 E and D
EECKHOUT, GERBRANDT VAN DEN
26 *Christ in the Synagogue at Nazareth*, 1658 (National Gallery of Ireland, Dublin) 19 E; **27** *The Prophet Elisha and the Shunammite Woman*, 1664 (Szépmüveszeti Museum, Budapest) 61 D
EVERDINGEN, CAESAR VAN
28 *The Glorification of the Burgomasters of Amsterdam* (Kunsthalle, Hamburg) 18 E
EYCK, JAN VAN
29 *Giovanni Arnolfini and his Wife*, 1434 (National Gallery, London) 6 E and D, 7 D
FABRITIUS, BARENT
30 *Peter in the House of Cornelius*, 1635 (Duke Anton Ulrich Museum, Brunswick) 61 E
FABRITIUS, CAREL
31 *The Goldfinch*, 1654 (Mauritshuis, The Hague) 57 E; **32** *Portrait of Abraham de Potter*, c.1648 (RA) 61 E
FLEURY, ROBERT
33 *Galileo before the Holy Office*, 1847 (Louvre, Paris) 29 E
FLINCK, GOVAERT
34 *Portrait of Rembrandt*, c.1633 (Gemäldegalerie, Berlin) 60 E; **35** *Portrait of Rembrandt*, 1636 (RA) 24 E
HALS, FRANS
36 *Banquet of the Officers of the Militia Company of St George*, 1616 (Frans Halsmuseum, Haarlem) 24 E; **37** *Couple Out of Doors*, c.1621 (RA) 24 E; **38** *Hille Bobbe*, c.1630 (Musée des Beaux-Arts, Lille) 25 E; **39** *The Merry Toper*, 1657 (RA) 25 E; **40** *Portrait of Nicolaes Hasselaer*, c.1635 (RA) 24 D
HEDA, WILLEM CLAESZ
41 *Luncheon with Lobsters*, 1648 (Hermitage, St Petersburg) 57 E and D; **42** *Still Life*, 1634 (BMR) 57 E and D

HEYDEN, JAN VAN DER
43 *Blazing House*, from the Brandspuitenboeck (HMA) 44 E; **44** *View of the Town Hall* (Louvre, Paris) 32 D
HONDECOETER, MELCHIOR
45 *Peacocks and Ducks*, 1680 (Wallace Collection, London) 56 E
HOOGH, PIETER DE
46 *Courtyard of a House in Delft*, 1658 (Noortman Gallery, London) 45 E; **47** *The Linen Cupboard*, 1658 (RA) 44 E
HOOGSTRATEN, SAMUEL VAN
48 *Interior of a Dutch House*, magic box, 1650 (National Gallery, London) 31 E; **49** *Self-portrait*, 1645 (Prince of Lichtenstein Collection, Vaduz) 60 E
JOUDERVILLE, ISAAK
50 *Bust of Young Man*, c.1631 (National Gallery of Ireland, Dublin) 60 E
KALFF, WILLEM
51 *Still Life*, c.1650 (Mauritshuis, The Hague) 56 E, 57 D
KEYSER, THOMAS DE
52 *The Anatomy Lesson of Doctor Egbertsz* (HMA) 35 E
LAIRESSE, GÉRARD DE
53 *The Peoples of the World Paying Homage to Amsterdam*, c.1670-80 (HMA) 18 D, 19 E
LASTMAN, PIETER
54 *Deposition*, c.1620 (Musée des Beaux-Arts, Lille) 18 E; **55** *Susanna and the Elders*, 1614 (Gemäldegalerie, Berlin) 19 D
LIEVENS, JAN
56 *Pilate Washing his Hands*, 1625-30 (Lakenhal, Leiden) 18 E
LYON, JACOB
57 *Captain Hoogkame's Company* (HMA) 25 D
MAES, NICOLAES
58 *Portrait of Jacob Trip*, 1659-60 (Mauritshuis, The Hague) 61 E
MANTEGNA, ANDREA
59 *Dead Christ*, before 1506 (Brera, Milan) 35 E
MEMLING, HANS
60 *St John the Evangelist Altarpiece*, 1479 (Memling Museum, Bruges) 6 E, 7 D
MICKER, JAN CHRISTIAENSZ
61 *View of Amsterdam* (HMA) 32 E
MIEREVELD, PIETER VAN
62 *The Anatomy Lesson of Doctor van der Meer* (Gemeentemuseum, Delft) 35 E
MIERIS, FRANS VAN
63 *Portrait of Woman with Parrot* (National Gallery, London) 25 E; **64** *Two Old People at Table*, 1655-60 (Uffizi, Florence) 45 E
MOSTAERT, GILLIS
65 *The Sack of a Village*, late sixteenth century (KMV) 9 E
OSTADE, ADRIAEN VAN
66 *Peasant Gathering*, 1661 (RA) 45 D
OSTERWYCK, MARIA VAN
67 *Flowers, Fruit, Insects* (Palatine Gallery, Florence) 56 E
PAX, H.A.
68 *The Princes of Orange in the Buitenhof at The Hague* (Mauritshuis, The Hague) 24 D
PETRUS CHRISTUS
69 *Portrait of Young Girl*, c.1445 (Staatliche Museen, Berlin) 6 E
POTTER, PAULUS
70 *The Bull*, 1647 (Mauritshuis, The Hague) 33 E
REMBRANDT
71 *The Anatomy Lesson of Doctor Deyman*, 1656 (HMA) 35 E; **72** preliminary sketch for *The Anatomy Lesson of Doctor Deyman* (HMA) 34 E; **73** *The Anatomy Lesson of Doctor Tulp*, 1632 (Mauritshuis, The Hague) 34 E and D, 35 D; **74** *Anna and Tobit*, 1626 (RA) 20 E and D, 21 D; **75** *Balaam's Ass*, 1626 (Cognaq-Jay Museum, Paris) 19 E; **76** *Child and Dead Peacocks*, c.1639 (RA) 57 E; **77** *Family Portrait*, 1668-69 (Duke Anton Ulrich Museum, Brunswick) 59 E; **78** *Faust*, engraving, 1652 53 E; **79** *The Jewish Bride*, 1662-64 (RA) 58 E, 59 D; **80** *Landscape with Bridge*, c.1640 (RA) 33 E; **81** *The Night Watch*, 1642 (RA) 50 E and D, 51 D; **82** *The Painter's Studio*, c.1648 (Louvre, Paris) 48 E; **83** *Portrait of Couple in an Interior*, 1633 (Isabella Stewart Gardner Museum, Boston) 27 E; **84** *Portrait of Hendrickje*, c.1654 (Louvre, Paris) 46 E; **85** *Portrait of Jacob de Gheyn III*, 1632 (Dulwich Art Gallery, London) 21 E, 26 E and D; **86** *Portrait of Maria Trip*, 1639 (RA) 26 E; **87** *Portrait of Maurits Huygens*, 1632 (Hamburger Kunsthalle, Hamburg) 26 D, 27 E and D; **88** *Portrait of Philip Lucasz*, 1635 (National Gallery, London) 37 E; **89** *Portrait of Seated Man*, c. 1632 (KMV) 27 E; **90** *Portrait of Seated Woman*, c.1632 (KMV) 27 E; **91** *Portrait of Titus*, c.1660 (Louvre, Paris) 58 E; **92** *Portrait of Well-dressed Young Man*, c.1665 (Montreal Museum of Fine Arts, Montreal) 58 E; **93** *Rembrandt's Father*, c.1630-31 (Mauritshuis, The Hague) 46 E; **94** *Rembrandt's Mother*, 1631 (RA) 46 E; **95** *Rembrandt's Mother with her Hand on her Chest*, engraving, 1631 (Bibliothèque

Nationale, Paris) 20 E; **96** *Saskia*, drawing, c. 1640 (Musée Bonnat, Bayonee) 46 E; **97** *Saskia in Arcadian Costume*, 1635 (National Gallery, London) 46 E; **98** *Self-portrait*, c.1628 (RA) 54 E; **99** *Self-portrait*, 1629 (RA) 54 E; **100** *Self-portrait*, c.1629 (Mauritshuis, The Hague) 54 E; **101** *Self-portrait*, 1630 (Bibliothèque Nationale, Paris) 54 E; **102** *Self-portrait*, c.1662 (Uffizi, Florence) 54 E; **103** *Self-portrait*, c.1665 (Kenwood House, London) 54 E; **104** *Self-portrait at the Age of 34*, 1640 (National Gallery, London) 54 E; **105** *Self-portrait in Fancy Clothing*, 1635-36 (Mauritshuis, The Hague) 55 E; **106** *Self-portrait* or *The Prodigal Son in the Tavern*, c.1635 (Gemäldegalerie, Dresden) 55 E; **107** *Study for The Jewish Bride*, pen drawing, c.1635 (Nasional Museet, Stockholm) 58 E; **108** *Study of a Head*, ink drawing, c. 1636 (Barber Institute, Birmingham) 20 D; **109** *Titus as a Monk*, 1660 (RA) 47 D; **110** *Tobit Accusing Anna of Stealing the Kid*, 1645 (Gemäldegalerie, Berlin) 21 E; **111** *View of Amsterdam* (RA) 33 E; **112** *Windmill*, engraving, 1641 (RA) 53 E
REMBRANDT (ATTRIB.)
113 *Self-portrait*, 1639-40 (Uffizi, Florence) 55 E; **114** *Self-portrait* or *Portrait of Rembrandt in Oriental Costume with Poodle*, c.1631 (Petit Palais, Paris) 55 E
REMBRANDT (WORKSHOP)
115 *Master and Pupils Drawing from Life*, engraving (Landesmuseum, Darmstadt) 60 E
RUBENS, PETER PAUL
116 *The Miracles of St Ignatius Loyola*, 1618-19 (KMV) 9 E; **117** *Portrait of Albert of Austria*, 1613-15 (KMV) 8 E; **118** *Portrait of Isabella of Habsburg* (KMV) 8 E; **119** *Self-portrait with his Wife Isabella*, 1609-10 (Alte Pinakothek, Munich) 8 E; **120** *Self-portrait*, c.1649 (KMV) 9 E
RUYSDAEL, JACOB VAN
121 *View of Haarlem* (Gemäldegalerie, Berlin) 33 E
RUYSDAEL, SALOMON
122 *Landscape with River*, 1649 (RA) 33 E
SAENREDAM, PIETER
123 *Church of St Adolf at Assenfeld*, 1649 (RA) 9 E; **124** *Interior of St Bavo's, Haarlem*, 1635 (RA) 45 E; **125** *Interior of St Lawrence Church, Alkmaar*, 1661 (BMR) 44 E
SCHOOR, ABRAHAM VAN DER
126 *Vanitas* (RA) 57 E
STEEN, JAN
127 *The Cabaret*, 1660-70 (Mauritshuis, The Hague) 44 D; **128** *The Prince's Birthday*, 1660-70 (HMA) 45 E
SWANEVELT, HERMAN VAN
129 *Landscape with Figures*, c.1640 (Uffizi, Florence) 32 D
TER BORCH, GERARD
130 *Self-portrait*, c.1670 (Mauritshuis, The Hague) 25 E
TITIAN
131 Study for *Martyrdom of St Peter* (Louvre, Paris) 47 E; **132** *Pietà*, 1570-76 (Accademia Gallery, Venice) 59 E
VALCKERT, WERNER VAN DE
133 *Distribution of Bread at the Almoezeniershuis*, 1627 (HMA) 29 E
VELDE, JAN VAN DE
134 *Anna and Tobit*, engraving from a drawing done by Buytewech in 1629 (Rijksprentenkabinett, Amsterdam) 21 E
VELDE, WILLEM VAN DE
135 *The Port of Amsterdam*, 1686 (HMA) 33 D
VERMEER, JAN
136 *The Artist's Studio*, c. 1665 (KMV) 38 D, 40 E and D; **137** *The Astronomer*, c.1668 (Louvre, Paris) 38 D, 41 E; **138** *The Geographer*, c.1668 (Städelsches Kunstinstitut, Berlin) 39 E and D, 40 E; **139** *The Glass of Wine*, 1660-61 (Gemäldegalerie, Berlin) 41 E; **140** *Lady at the Virginals*, c.1670 (National Gallery, London) 41 D; **141** *The Music Lesson*, 1664 (Buckingham Palace, London) 31 E; **142** *Woman with a Pearl Necklace*, 1662-65 (Gemäldegalerie, Berlin) 41 E; **143** *Woman Reading a Letter*, 1662-65 (RA) 41 E; **144** *View of Delft*, 1661 (Mauritshuis, The Hague) 41 E
VICTORS, JAN
145 *Joseph Recounting his Dreams*, 1651 (Kunstmuseum, Düsseldorf) 61 E
VISSCHER, CLAES
146 *View of the Port of Amsterdam*, engraving, 1630 (private collection) 11 D
VROOM, HENDRICK
147 *The Port of Amsterdam* (Schlessheim Castle, Bavaria) 32 D
WITTE, EMANUEL DE
148 *Church Interior*, 1617-22 (Musée Jeanne d'Aboville, La Fere) 45 E
WOUWERMAN, PHILIPS
149 *Battle Scene*, 1650 (National Gallery, London) 19 E

◆ INDEX

A

Albert of Austria, archduke 8
Amsterdam 11, 22-23, 28, 37, 38
- Amstel river 15, 22, 23
- Bank of Amsterdam 14
- guilds 15
- musketeers 50-51
- Nieuwe Kerk 14, 23
- origins 23
- stock exchange 14, 23
- town hall 14, 23
anatomy theaters 34, 35
Avercamp, Hendrick 33

B

Banning Cocq, Frans 5, 50
Berckheyde, Job Adriaensz 14
Beyeren, Abraham van 56
Blaeu, Willem Jansz 16, 17, 38
Bol, Ferdinand 18, 19, 24-25, 29, 61
booksellers 16-17, 38
Bosch, Hieronymus 7
Bosschaert the Elder, Ambrosius 56-57
Braun, Georg 38
Bruegel the Elder, Pieter 7

C

Calvinism 10, 24, 44
camera obscura 30, 31
Canaletto, byname of Giovanni Antonio Canal 30
cartography 16, 17, 32, 38-39
censorship 16, 28
Christus, Petrus 6
Claesz, Pieter 56

D

Descartes, René 16, 22
Dircx, Geertge 42
Dort, Synod of 28
Dou, Gerrit 21, 22, 60

Dreyer, Carl Theodor 35
Drost, Willem 61
Dürer, Albrecht 52
Dutch East India Company 16, 17, 36, 37, 39
Dyck, Anthony van 9, 24, 27

E

Eeckhout, Gerbrandt van den 18-19, 61
Elzevier, Louis 16
engraving 52
etching 52-53
Everdingen, Caesar van 18
Eyck, Jan van 6, 7

F

Fabritius, Barent 61
Fabritius, Carel 56-57, 61
Flemish art 6-7, 24
Flinck, Govaert 24, 53, 60
fluyt 36
Frederick Henry, Prince of Orange 5, 28

G

Galileo Galilei 16, 28, 29
genre painting 44-45
Gheyn III, Jacob de 26, 27
Goyen, Jan van 57
Guercino, byname of Giovanni Francesco Barbieri 48
guilds 14

H

Haarlem school 24
Hals, Frans 5, 24, 25
Heda, Willem Claesz 56, 57
Heyden, Jan van der 32, 44
history painting 18-19
Hogenberg, Frans 38
Holland
- architecture 42-43
- Calvinist 24
- canals 10, 11, 42
- dikes 22
- Golden Age 4, 10-11, 16

- homes 42-43
- polders 22
- shipbuilding 11, 36, 37
- States General 14, 28
- tolerance 28-29
- trading nation 10-11, 36-37
- United Provinces 8, 10, 28
see also Amsterdam
Hondecoeter, Melchior 56
Hondius 17, 38
Hoogstraten, Samuel van 31, 51, 60
Huygens, Constantijn 4, 22, 26, 28
Huygens, Maurits 26, 27

I

Inquisition 8, 9
interiors 44-45
Isabella of Habsburg 8

J

Jouderville, Isaak 60

K

Kalff, Willem 56
Keyser, Thomas de 35

L

Lairesse, Gérard de 18-19, 59
landscape painting 32-33
Lastman, Pieter 18-19
Leeuwenhoek, Antony van 28
Leiden 12-13, 35
Lievens, Jan 4, 18, 22
Loo, Magdalena van 58, 59, 60
Lyon, Jacob 24-25

M

Maes, Nicolaes 61
Manhattan 39
maps, *see* cartography
Memling, Hans 6, 7
Micker, Jan Christiaensz 32
microscope 28, 30

middle classes 14-15, 18, 24, 32, 44
Miereveld, Pieter van 35
Mieris, Frans van 24-25, 44-45
Moluccas 39

N

Netherlands, Spanish 8-9, 16

O

optics 30
Orange, house of 28
Ostade, Adriaen van 44-45
Osterwyck, Maria van 56

P

Pax, H.A. 24
portraiture 24-25, 26-27
Potter, Paulus 32-33
printers 17

R

religious paintings 18-19
Rembrandt
- etchings 53
- and film directors 35
- landscapes 32-33
- parents 4, 13, 17, 22, 46
- portraiture 26-27, 34, 35, 37, 46, 47, 50, 51, 58, 59
- self-portraits 50, 54-55
- signature 21
- still life 57
- workshop 48-49, 60-61
Rubens, Peter Paul 5, 8, 9
Ruysdael, Jacob van 32-33
Ruysdael, Salomon van 32-33
Ryther, Augustine 38

S

Saenredam, Pieter 9, 44, 45
Saskia, *see* Uylenburgh, Saskia van
Schoor, Abraham van der 57

Spain, Spanish rule of Netherlands 8
Spinoza, Baruch 5, 28, 29
Stadholders 28
Steen, Jan 44-45, 57
still life 56-57
Stoffels, Hendrickje 4, 42, 46, 48, 53, 56, 58
Swanenburgh, Jacob van 18
Swanevelt, Herman van 32

T

Ter Borch, Gerard 24-25
theodolite 38
Titian, Tiziano Vecellio 47, 59
Titus 4, 42, 46, 47, 48, 53, 58, 60
tulip mania 14, 15
Tulp, Dr Nicolaes Pietersz 5, 34, 35

U

United Provinces, *see* Holland
Uylenburgh, Hendrick van 4, 22, 28
Uylenburgh, Saskia van 4, 28, 32, 42, 46, 55

V

Valckert, Werner van de 29
Vanitas 57
Velde, Willem van de 32-33, 57
Vermeer, Jan 5, 28, 30, 31, 38, 39, 40-41
Victors, Jan 61
Visscher, Claes 11
Vroom, Hendrick 32

W

windmills 12-13, 22
witch-hunts 29
Witte, Emanuel de 44-45
woodcut 52
Wouwerman, Philips 18-19

◆ CREDITS

(Abbreviations: b, bottom; c, center; l, left; r, right; t, top)
The original and previously unpublished illustrations in this book may be reproduced only with the prior permission of Donati Giudici Associati, who hold the copyright.
The illustrations are by: Sergio (pp 4-5, 10-11, 12-13, 15b, 15t, 29c, 30-31, 42-43, 46-47, 48-49, 52-53); Paola Holguin (pp 11b, 12t, 13t, 15c, 27b, 29t, 30cl, 43tc, 43tr, 43cr, 52tl); Sebastiano Ranchetti (pp 8t, 9t, 10t, 22-23t, 28b); Andrea Ricciardi (pp 14-15); Thomas Trojer (pp 36-37). Cover picture: Sergio.
Alinari/Bridgeman/Giraudon: 46; Alinari/Giraudon: 25, 38, 44, 62, 82, 114, 125, 147, 148; Alinari/Lauros/Giraudon: 84, 96, 148; Archivio Giunti, Florence: 19, 27, 49; Archivio Scala, Florence: 9, 41, 132, 137; Artephot: 75, 77, 101; Artephot/Artoteque: 13; Artephot/A. Held: 87; Artephot/G. Reinold: 106;

Artephot/Nimatallah: 59; Atlas van Stolk, Rotterdam: 5, 6; Bibliothèque Nationale, Paris: 1; Boymans-van Beuningen Museum, Rotterdam/Tom Haartsen: 8, 22, 42; Bridgeman Art Library: 45, 70, 85, 93, 103, 104, 105, 108, 138, 140, 149; Bridgeman/Giraudon: 54; Doge's Palace, Venice: 16; DR: 146; Duke Anton Ulrich Museum, Brunswick: 36; Erich Lessing, Vienna: 17, 18, 29, 36, 60, 65, 73, 89, 90, 91, 97, 116, 117, 118, 119, 120, 136, 144; Hamburger Kunsthaus, Hamburg: 28; Hessisches Landesmuseum, Darmstadt: 115; Historisch Museum, Amsterdam: 10, 11, 12, 15, 43, 52, 53, 57, 61, 71, 72, 128, 133, 135; Isabella Stewart Gardner Museum, Boston: 83; Kunstmuseum in Ehrenhof, Düsseldorf: 145; Lakenhal, Leiden: 56; Mauritshaus, The Hague: 31, 51, 58, 68, 100, 127, 130; Museum of Fine Arts, Montreal: 92; Nasional Museet, Stockholm: 107; National Gallery, London: 21, 48, 63, 88; National Gallery of Ireland, Dublin: 26, 50;

Rijksmuseum, Amsterdam: 2, 7, 14, 20, 32, 35, 37, 39, 40, 47, 66, 74, 76, 78, 79, 80, 81, 86, 94, 98, 99, 109, 111, 112, 122, 123, 124, 126, 134, 143; RMN: 33, 131; Roger-Viollet: 24, 95; Serge Dominge/Marco Rabatti: 64, 67, 102, 113, 129; Staatliche Museen Preußischer Kulturbesitz, Berlin/Jörg P. Anders: 23, 34, 55, 69, 110, 121, 139, 142; The Royal Collection, Her Majesty Queen Elizabeth II, London: 141; University Library, Amsterdam: 4.
Documents: DoGi Archive: pp 35tr, 38cr, 38cl, 39tr, 39br; Museo della Scienza, Florence: pp 38b, 39t; Alinari/Giraudon: pp 16bl, 16br; Roger-Viollet: pp 21cr, 42t.

DoGi s.r.l. have made every effort to trace other possible copyright holders. If any omissions have been made, this will be corrected at reprint.